Goose berry Patch co.

A Country Store In Your Mailbox®

Taste of Autumn

Filled to the brim with harvest celebrations, tasty recipes and fun for the whole family!

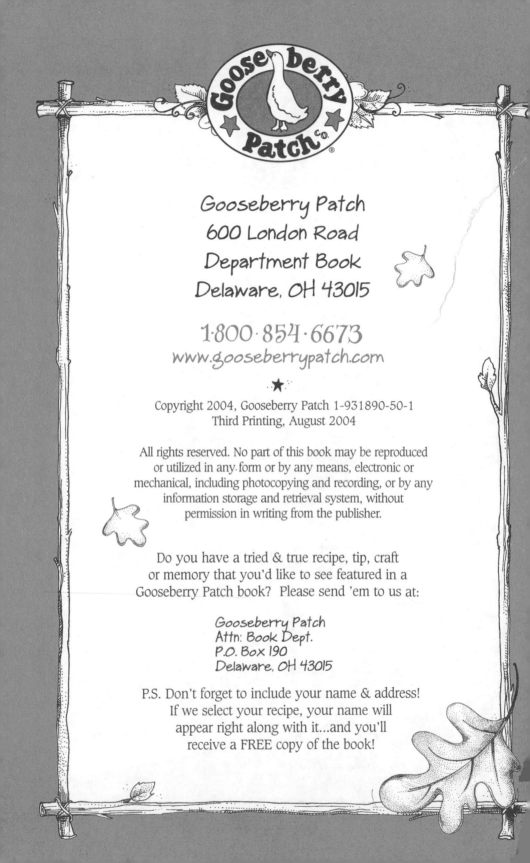

Gooseberry Patch
600 London Road
Department Book
Delaware, OH 43015

1·800·854·6673
www.gooseberrypatch.com

★

Do you have a tried & true recipe, tip, craft
or memory that you'd like to see featured in a
Gooseberry Patch book? Please send 'em to us at:

Gooseberry Patch
Attn: Book Dept.
P.O. Box 190
Delaware, OH 43015

P.S. Don't forget to include your name & address!
If we select your recipe, your name will
appear right along with it...and you'll
receive a FREE copy of the book!

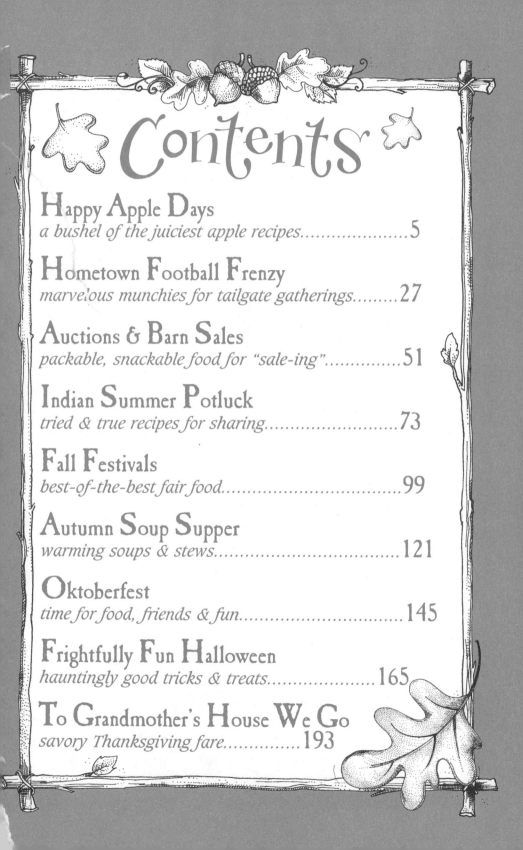

Contents

Dedication and Appreciation

To all who delight in crunchy red apples, woolly sweaters, plump pumpkins and crackling fires…this book is dedicated to you!

A very special "Thanks" to all who inspire us to create a homespun harvest!

Apple-Walnut Coffee Cake

*Jessica Parker
Mulvane, KS*

A moist and yummy cake that freezes so well.

2-1/2 c. all-purpose flour
1-1/2 c. brown sugar, packed
3/4 c. butter, softened
1 c. chopped walnuts, toasted
1 t. baking soda
1 t. cinnamon
1/2 t. salt
1 egg
3/4 c. sour cream
1 t. vanilla extract
2 apples, cored, peeled and
    chopped

Combine flour, brown sugar and butter with a fork until crumbly; stir in nuts. Divide mixture in half. Press one half into the bottom of a buttered 9-1/2" springform baking pan to form crust; set aside. Add baking soda, cinnamon and salt to remaining crumb mixture; mix well. Make a well in the center; set aside. Beat egg with sour cream and vanilla in a small bowl until smooth; add to flour mixture, stirring until just combined. Fold in apples; spread batter evenly over crust. Bake at 375 degrees for one hour and 20 minutes or until cake tests done; cool in pan on a wire rack. Makes 12 servings.

A mini dried-apple wreath makes a fragrant, fall napkin
ring...ready in seconds!

Honey-Baked Apples & Pears

Kathy Grashoff
Fort Wayne, IN

Try this honey-glazed treat for breakfast or dessert.

2 apples, cored, peeled and
    sliced into 8 wedges
1 pear, cored, peeled and sliced
    into 8 wedges
2/3 c. honey

2 T. water
1-1/2 t. cinnamon
3 T. butter, sliced

Arrange apples and pears in a greased one-quart baking dish; set aside. Combine honey, water and cinnamon; pour over apple mixture. Dot with butter; bake at 350 degrees for 25 minutes or until fruit is tender. Serves 4.

Use caramel apples as festive placecards...rubber stamp a mailing tag, then tie onto the apple's stick with ribbon or raffia.

Cinnamon-Apple Blintzes

Jennifer Niemi
Nova Scotia, Canada

Can you think of a more delicious way to start a crisp autumn morning than with these? After breakfast, everyone in our family heads out to rake leaves, plant spring bulbs or enjoy a long hike through the country. In fact, we think it might just be the start to a perfect day!

1/3 c. butter, divided
1 c. all-purpose flour
1/2 c. sugar, divided
1/2 t. salt
2 eggs
1-1/3 c. milk
1 t. vanilla extract

3 c. Granny Smith apples, cored, peeled and diced
1 T. lemon juice
2 t. cinnamon
1/4 t. nutmeg
1 T. cornstarch
Garnish: sugar

Melt 3 tablespoons butter. Combine flour, 3 tablespoons sugar, salt, eggs, milk, melted butter and vanilla in a large bowl. Blend until thoroughly combined and slightly frothy. Cover with plastic wrap; set aside for 45 minutes. Pour 1/2 cup batter into a 7-1/2" skillet sprayed with non-stick vegetable spray; tilt skillet to coat the bottom evenly with batter. Cook until edges are firm and batter loses its shine; turn carefully and cook other side for one minute. Remove to serving platter; keep warm. Repeat with remaining batter to make 6 crepes. Combine apples, lemon juice, remaining sugar, spices and cornstarch in a medium saucepan. Stir well and cook over medium-high heat for 10 minutes, stirring constantly until mixture thickens and apples soften. Place a generous portion of apple mixture in the center of each crepe. Fold the top and bottom of crepes over filling, then fold in sides. Melt remaining butter in a large heavy skillet; arrange filled crepes in skillet, folded-sides down. Sauté for 7 to 10 minutes or until golden and slightly crisp. Turn and repeat on other side. Sprinkle with sugar; serve warm. Makes 6 servings.

8

German Apple Pancake

Linda Charles
Oconomowoc, WI

*I love to serve this pancake as a special breakfast for 2 or
a warm dessert for 4...it's a no-fail recipe!*

3 eggs
3/4 c. milk
3/4 c. all-purpose flour
1/2 t. salt
1-3/4 T. butter, divided

3-1/2 c. Golden Delicious apples,
   cored, peeled and sliced,
   divided
1/4 c. sugar
cinnamon and nutmeg to taste

Blend eggs, milk, flour and salt; stir in 1/2 cup apples. Melt
1-1/2 tablespoons butter in a 12" oven-proof skillet. When very hot,
pour in egg mixture and place skillet in oven at 450 degrees for
15 minutes. Reduce temperature to 350 degrees and bake for an
additional 10 minutes. While pancake is baking, melt remaining butter
in a second skillet; sauté remaining apples just until tender, 8 to
10 minutes. Sprinkle apples with sugar, cinnamon and nutmeg; spread
over warm pancake. Cut in wedges to serve. Makes 4 servings.

What are the best apples for baking? Try using juicy Golden
Delicious or tangy Jonagold!

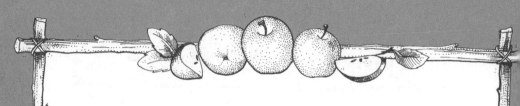

Fruit-Stuffed Cornish Game Hens

Karla Harrington
Anchorage, AK

My mother always prepared this on Christmas Eve, but it can be enjoyed any time of year.

4 c. water
1 c. orange juice
2 T. butter
2 6-oz. pkgs. long grain and
   wild rice mix

1 c. celery, diced
1 c. pitted dates, chopped
1 c. dried apples, chopped
1/2 c. dried apricots, chopped
4 to 6 Cornish game hens

Place water, orange juice and butter in a saucepan; stir in rice mix, including seasoning packets. Bring to a boil; cover and cook for 20 to 22 minutes. Stir in celery, dates, apples and apricots. Stuff game hens loosely with mixture; arrange hens in a very large roasting pan. Bake at 350 degrees for one hour to one hour and 15 minutes, basting every 1/2 hour. Serves 4 to 6.

An autumn picnic means the tablecloth may flutter in the breeze. Keep in place by tying jute around an apple stem, then laying it across the table. Secure a second apple at the other end...so simple!

Brown Sugar Pork Chops

Maureen Livingston
Clifton Park, NY

I like this served with a side of prepared white or brown rice.

4 pork chops, browned
4 potatoes, cubed
3 apples, cored and cubed

1/2 onion, chopped
1 t. cinnamon
2 T. brown sugar, packed

Arrange pork chops in an 8"x8" baking dish. Top with potatoes, apples and onion; sprinkle with cinnamon and brown sugar. Cover and bake at 350 degrees for one hour or until tender. Serves 4.

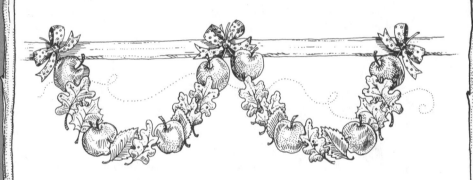

A garland of apples and leaves dresses up a front porch with a blaze of color! Use an awl to pierce holes horizontally through apples, then string them on jute. Knot the jute on each side to hold the apples in place and alternate apples with bunches of fresh, colorful leaves.

Sweet Potato-Apple Bake

Wendy Jacobs
Idaho Falls, ID

A tasty new spin on traditional sweet potato casserole.

4 sweet potatoes, boiled, peeled
    and sliced
1/2 c. butter
4 tart apples, cored, peeled and
    sliced
1/2 c. sugar

1/2 c. brown sugar, packed
1 to 2 t. cinnamon
1/2 c. water
1/4 c. lemon juice
1/4 c. orange juice

Arrange a layer of sliced potatoes in a greased one-quart baking dish;
dot with butter and sprinkle with sugar, brown sugar and cinnamon.
Arrange a layer of apple slices on top; continue layering until all
ingredients are used. Combine water and juices; sprinkle over top.
Cover and bake at 400 degrees for 45 minutes or until apples are
tender. Makes 4 to 6 servings.

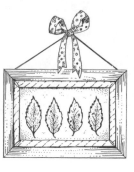

It's time to pull on a sweater and head outdoors on a
leaf-collecting expedition! Press the most beautiful leaves
between the pages of a book and in a few days, when they've
flattened and dried a bit, slip them between the panes of
glass-backed frames. Sheets of paper, carefully torn on the
edges, make a simple mat.

Sweet & Spicy Pork Ribs

Cheri Reeves
Coral Springs, FL

A slow-cooker recipe that can't be beat.

1-lb. pkg. boneless pork ribs, cut
    into 1"x2" portions
1/4 c. all-purpose flour
1 t. garlic salt
1/2 t. pepper
1/2 T. paprika

1 T. browning and seasoning
    sauce
2 onions, sliced
2 Granny Smith apples, cored,
    quartered and sliced
1/4 c. brown sugar, packed

Place meat in a plastic zipping bag; add flour, garlic salt, pepper and paprika and shake to coat. Arrange in a slow cooker; drizzle with browning sauce and top with onions. Cook on low setting for 4 to 6 hours. During final hour of cooking, arrange apples on top and sprinkle with brown sugar; continue cooking until meat and apples are tender. Serves 4.

A centerpiece in a snap! Nestle a plump candle in the center of a simple glass salad or punch bowl, then fill around it with small apples.

Apple-Acorn Squash

Gail Prather
Bethel, MN

*I always plant squash in my summer garden to enjoy
in this dish during the summer and fall months.*

2 acorn squash, halved and
    seeds removed
1/2 c. apple juice
1/4 c. butter, melted

1/4 t. nutmeg
2 T. brown sugar, packed
1 t. orange zest
2 tart apples, cored and sliced

Place squash cut side-up in a 13"x9" baking pan; pour apple juice on
top and set aside. Combine butter, nutmeg, brown sugar and zest in a
bowl. Divide apple slices evenly among squash halves; pour butter
mixture over apples. Cover and bake at 375 degrees for 45 to
50 minutes. Serves 4.

It's easy to dry apples for crafting fall decorations, just slice
apples 1/8-inch thick across the core and soak for
20 minutes in a mixture of 2 cups lemon juice and
3 tablespoons salt. Pat apple slices dry and arrange in a single
layer on baking sheets. Sprinkle with ground cinnamon and
ground cloves, then bake in a 150-degree oven for about
6 hours or until they feel and look leathery.

Baked Apple & Carrot Casserole

Mary Brown
Sayre, PA

A family favorite we serve alongside ham.

6 apples, cored, peeled, sliced
   and divided
2 c. carrots, sliced, cooked and
   divided

1/3 c. brown sugar, packed
2 T. all-purpose flour
salt to taste
3/4 c. orange juice

Arrange half the apples in a greased 2-quart casserole; cover with half the carrots. Repeat layers; sprinkle with sugar, flour and salt. Pour orange juice over the top; bake at 350 degrees for 45 minutes. Makes 6 servings.

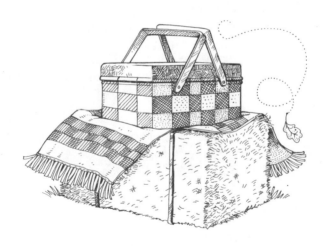

Plan a trip to the local apple orchard for a fall outing...swirling leaves and the sweet smell of apples make it the ideal picnic spot! Toss a couple sawhorses and length of plywood in the back of a truck for a fast picnic table and borrow a few straw bales for seating.

Butternut Squash & Apple Soup

Angela Murphy
Tempe, AZ

Search flea markets for pretty apple-shaped bowls to ladle this savory soup into.

2 slices bacon
1/2 c. onions, chopped
1 c. leeks, chopped
1/2 bay leaf
1 clove garlic, minced
salt and pepper to taste
2-1/2 c. chicken broth

1-1/4 lbs. butternut squash, peeled, seeded and cut into 1-inch pieces
1 Granny Smith apple, cored, peeled and chopped
Garnish: 2 T. sour cream and apples, chopped

Cook bacon in a large saucepan; remove bacon, crumble and set aside. Add the onion, leeks, bay leaf, garlic, salt and pepper to the bacon drippings; stir and sauté until soft. Add broth, squash and apple; simmer for 15 minutes or until tender. Remove and discard bay leaf. Purée the mixture in a blender. Pour into a saucepan; add water to thin as desired and stir in sour cream. Heat just until warmed through. Spoon into bowls; sprinkle with the reserved bacon. Garnish with a dollop of sour cream and a spoonful of chopped apples. Makes 4 servings.

Right next to jumping into a pile of leaves, kids like nothing more than bobbing for apples! An easy recipe for fun...fill a galvanized tub with water, toss in a dozen or so apples; add kids. The secret? Grabbing the apple stem in your teeth.

Happy Apple Days

Pumpkin-Apple Soup

Kathy Grashoff
Fort Wayne, IN

Spoon into hollowed-out Baby-Boo pumpkins for serving...so sweet.

2 T. butter
1 onion, diced
2 green apples, cored, peeled
   and diced
1 T. all-purpose flour
4 c. chicken broth
3 c. canned pumpkin
2 T. brown sugar, packed

1 t. cinnamon
1 t. nutmeg
1 t. ginger
1 c. apple juice
1/2 c. half-and-half
salt and pepper to taste
Garnish: pumpkin seeds, toasted

Melt butter in a saucepan; add onion and apples and sauté until soft. Stir in flour; stir and cook 2 to 3 minutes. Gradually whisk in broth; stir in pumpkin, sugar, cinnamon, nutmeg and ginger. Bring to a boil; reduce heat and simmer covered for 25 minutes. Transfer to a blender; purée until smooth. Return to pan; pour in apple juice, half-and-half, salt and pepper and heat until warmed through. Sprinkle individual bowls with pumpkin seeds. Serves 6.

Whenever we bite into a juicy apple, we have Johnny Appleseed to thank. History tells us he traveled westward planting seeds he had collected from cider presses in Pennsylvania. Why not celebrate his birthday on September 26th? A fun and tasty history lesson for the kids!

Crunchy Pecan Salad

Debra Dearie
Newtown, PA

A "gourmet" tasting salad that's a snap to prepare.

12-oz. pkg. shredded broccoli
  slaw mix
1-1/2 c. seedless red grapes,
  halved

1-1/2 c. apples, cored and
  chopped
1/2 c. citrus salad dressing
3/4 c. chopped pecans

Combine broccoli, grapes and apples in a serving bowl. Pour dressing on top; toss gently to coat. Sprinkle with pecans. Serves 6 to 8.

Tucking apples into lunchboxes? Try using tart Cortlands, sweet Crispins or spicy Fujis…all crunchy and perfect for eating fresh!

Nutty Spinach Salad

Barbara Vanarsdall
Hilliard, OH

Try substituting sweetened, dried cranberries for a tangy taste.

10-oz. pkg. baby spinach
2 Granny Smith apples, cored
   and chopped
1/2 c. cashews
1/4 c. golden raisins

1/4 c. sugar
1/4 c. cider vinegar
1/4 c. oil
1/4 t. garlic salt
1/4 t. celery salt

Combine spinach, apples, cashews and raisins in a serving bowl; set aside. Mix remaining ingredients in a jar; cover and shake vigorously. Pour over spinach mixture; toss to coat. Serves 6.

Whip up an after-school snack of Apple Smiles in minutes. Cut apples into wedges and spread peanut butter on one side of 2 wedges. Add a few mini marshmallows on the peanut butter and top with a second apple wedge, peanut butter-side down. It's a smile...the red part of the apple wedges is the lips and the marshmallows the teeth!

Apple Salad

Sandy Pittman
Granby, MO

*This salad makes a pretty presentation made with
a variety of apples in different colors.*

3/4 c. mayonnaise-type salad
   dressing
2 T. sugar

1/2 t. black walnut extract
1 c. celery, diced
4 c. apples, cored and diced

Blend mayonnaise and sugar together; add walnut extract. Fold celery
and apples into mixture; refrigerate for 2 hours. Serves 4 to 6.

Chances are there's a list of bike paths in your area. Gather
the family together and enjoy the fall colors on a tree-lined
path. Pack a thermos of icy cider to enjoy along the way.

Autumn Apple Salad

Tiera Lesley
Bartlesville, OK

Frosty and fluffy...just like Grandma makes!

20-oz. can crushed pineapple
1/4 c. sugar
3-oz. pkg. lemon gelatin mix
8-oz. pkg. cream cheese,
   softened
1 apple, cored and chopped

1/2 c. chopped nuts
1/2 c. celery, chopped
8-oz. container frozen whipped
   topping, thawed

Combine pineapple with juice and sugar in a saucepan; bring to a boil for 3 minutes, stirring often. Add gelatin and cream cheese; stir until mixture is combined. Remove from heat; cool, cover and refrigerate for one hour. Fold in apples, nuts and celery; mix in half of whipped topping, reserving other half for another use. Pour into a 2-quart baking dish; chill until firm. Serves 4.

A road like brown ribbon, a sky that is blue,
A forest of green, with the sky peeping through,
Asters, deep purple, a grasshopper's call,
Today it is summer, tomorrow is fall.

-Edwina Fallis

Apple Cake with Butter Sauce

Kris Warner
Circleville, OH

Topped with butter sauce, this cake is irresistible.

1/4 c. butter, softened
1 c. sugar
1 egg
1 t. vanilla extract
1 c. all-purpose flour
1 t. baking soda

1 t. cinnamon
1/4 t. salt
1/4 t. nutmeg
2 tart apples, cored, peeled and
  grated

Cream butter and sugar together. Beat in egg and vanilla and set aside. Combine flour, baking soda, cinnamon, salt, and nutmeg; gradually add to creamed mixture. Fold in apples. Pour into a greased 8"x8" baking pan. Bake at 350 degrees for 40 to 45 minutes. Serve warm with Butter Sauce. Makes 12 servings.

Butter Sauce:

1/2 c. butter
1/2 c. sugar

1/2 c. brown sugar, packed
1/2 c. half-and-half

Melt butter in a saucepan; stir in sugar, brown sugar and half-and-half. Bring to a boil over medium heat, stirring constantly. Reduce heat; simmer, uncovered, for 15 minutes, stirring occasionally.

If you're looking for a quick & easy dessert try this: slice apples and place in serving bowls, top with warm caramel sauce and sprinkle with chopped nuts. Delicious!

Cinnamon Apples

Wendy Lee Paffenroth
Pine Island, NY

An old-fashioned favorite everyone will love.

8 to 10 apples, cored, peeled and
    sliced
1/2 c. brown sugar, packed
1/2 c. sugar
1/4 c. butter

1/2 c. honey
1 t. vanilla extract
cinnamon to taste

Arrange apple slices in a 1-1/2 to 2-quart casserole dish; set aside. Heat sugars, butter and honey in a heavy saucepan until sugars dissolve; stir until bubbly. Remove from heat; stir in vanilla and set aside. Sprinkle apples with cinnamon; pour sugar mixture on top and stir gently until evenly coated. Cover with aluminum foil; bake at 400 degrees for 30 minutes or until apples are tender. Makes 8 servings.

When family & friends get together for an autumn barn party or picnic, dust off an old-fashioned double wash tub and put it to work! The roomy twin tubs are ideal for filling with ice and jugs of cider or bottles of soda and water.

Applesauce Cookies

Roberta Nichols
Sun Valley, NV

A favorite sweet treat with a tall glass of ice cold milk!

1 c. applesauce
1 t. baking soda
1/2 c. shortening
2 eggs
1/2 t. cinnamon
1/2 t. ground cloves
1/2 t. nutmeg

1/2 t. salt
2 c. all-purpose flour
1 c. sugar
1 c. chopped nuts
12-oz. pkg. semi-sweet choco-
    late chips

Blend applesauce and baking soda together; set aside. In a second bowl, combine shortening, sugar, and eggs; set aside. Blend together flour, cinnamon, cloves, nutmeg and salt in a large mixing bowl; blend in shortening mixture with flour mixture. Add applesauce mixture; stir in nuts and chocolate chips. Drop by teaspoonfuls onto ungreased baking sheets; bake at 350 degrees for 10 to 12 minutes. Makes 2 to 3 dozen.

An apple basket filled with Applesauce Cookies makes a
tasty teacher gift...tuck in a tiny slate board as a
clever gift tag!

Autumn Apple Pie

Amy Butcher
Columbus, GA

For variety, try a different type of apple each time you make this pie.
Cortlands and Pippins are wonderful, too.

6 Granny Smith apples, cored,
   peeled and thinly sliced
3 T. lemon juice
1/2 c. brown sugar, packed
1/2 c. plus 1 T. sugar, divided
2 t. cinnamon

1/4 t. nutmeg
3 T. all-purpose flour
1/4 c. butter, chilled and diced
9 caramels, unwrapped and
   quartered
2 9-inch pie crusts

Combine apples, lemon juice, brown sugar, 1/2 cup sugar, cinnamon, nutmeg, flour, butter and caramels. Stir until mixture evenly coats apples. Line a 9" pie plate with one pie crust; spoon filling into the crust. Cover with second crust; flute edges and vent as desired. Sprinkle remaining sugar over crust. Place on an aluminum foil-covered baking sheet. Bake at 375 degrees for 30 minutes; reduce heat to 350 degrees and bake an additional 20 minutes or until crust is golden. Makes 6 to 8 servings.

For a new twist on caramel apples, insert a cinnamon stick instead of a lollipop stick in the center!

Apple Bread

Tina Knotts
Gooseberry Patch

So yummy...be sure to make an extra loaf to share!

3 eggs, beaten
2 c. sugar
1 c. oil
1 T. vanilla extract
3 c. all-purpose flour

1 t. baking soda
1 t. cinnamon
3 to 4 apples, cored and chopped
1 c. chopped pecans

Combine eggs, sugar, oil and vanilla until well mixed. Combine flour, baking soda and cinnamon; stir into egg mixture. Fold in apples and pecans. Divide equally between 2 greased and floured 9"x5" loaf pans. Bake at 325 degrees for one hour and 10 minutes. Makes 2 loaves.

Handy apple hints...cakes will stay extra-moist if you cut an apple in half and store it with the cake, and if you're looking for a frozen treat, simply put a lollipop stick in a small paper cup filled with cider and freeze...yum!

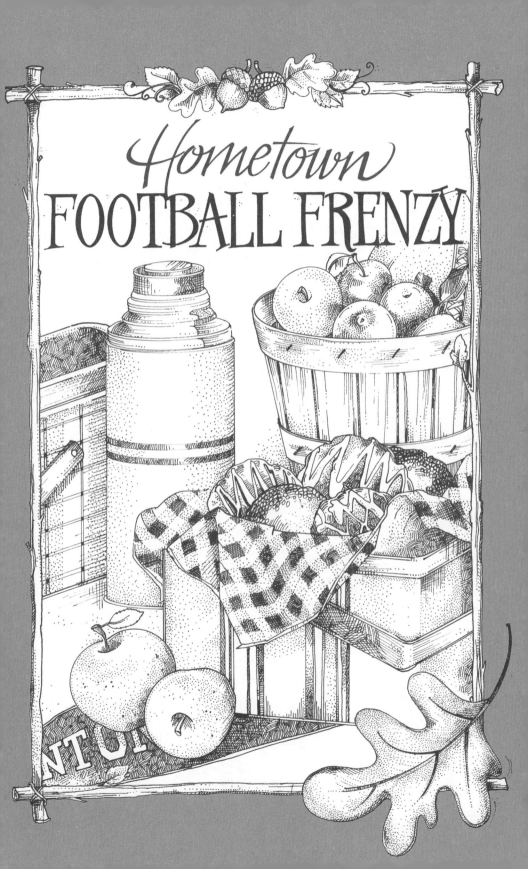

"Go Team, Go!" Cheese Ball

Anna McMaster
Portland, OR

Serve with apple slices and crispy crackers.

2 c. Havarti cheese, grated
8-oz. pkg. plus 3-oz. pkg. cream
   cheese, softened
1 t. dried thyme

1 t. dried chives
1 clove garlic, pressed
1/4 c. mayonnaise
yellow and red food coloring

Combine Havarti, cream cheese, thyme, chives and garlic; blend thoroughly. Shape into one cheese ball or divide in half to make 2 balls. Combine mayonnaise and enough food coloring to produce an orange color; frost cheese ball. Refrigerate until ready to serve. Makes 10 to 15 servings.

For tasty fun at the next tailgate party, turn any favorite cheese ball recipe into a "football." Just shape, sprinkle with paprika and pipe on sour cream or cream cheese "laces"...so easy!

Hometown Football Frenzy

Wild-Card Wings

Virginia Watson
Scranton, PA

Don't forget the dipping sauces...blue cheese dressing, honey mustard or barbecue sauce are all perfect.

2-1/2 c. potato chips, crushed
2 8-oz. cans French-fried
   onions, crushed
1/2 c. cornmeal
2 t. dried oregano
1 t. onion salt

1 t. garlic powder
1 t. paprika
2-1/2 lbs. chicken wings
2 eggs, beaten
1/4 c. butter, melted

Combine potato chips, onions, cornmeal and seasonings in a large plastic zipping bag; mix well. Dip chicken wings in eggs; place in bag, a few at a time. Shake to coat and press crumb mixture onto wings. Arrange in a greased jelly-roll pan; drizzle with butter. Bake, uncovered, at 375 degrees for 30 to 35 minutes or until juices run clear and coating is crisp. Makes about 2 dozen.

Invite friends over for a cookout before the big rivalry football game. Begin with invitations made out of felt in the shape of pennants or use a permanent marker to write party information on small plastic footballs.

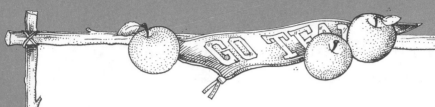

Touchdown Chile Relleno Squares

Kelly Wulff
Truckee, CA

Served hot or cold, this appetizer will score big!

1/2 c. all-purpose flour
1 t. baking powder
3/4 t. salt
8 eggs, beaten
1-1/2 c. cottage cheese

5 c. shredded Monterey Jack
    cheese, divided
4-oz. can diced green chiles
4-oz. can diced jalapeños
2 c. shredded Pepper Jack cheese

Stir together flour, baking powder and salt; add eggs. Fold in cottage cheese, 3 cups Monterey Jack cheese, green chiles, and half of jalapeños (reserving other half for another use). Spread in a greased 13"x9" baking pan. Bake at 350 degrees for 40 minutes; remove from oven. Combine remaining Monterey Jack cheese with Pepper Jack cheese; sprinkle on top. Set aside to cool to room temperature; slice into squares. Makes 2 to 3 dozen.

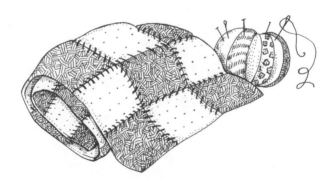

Nighttime football games can be chilly…stitch together a fleece lap blanket in team colors to keep cozy & warm. Fleece doesn't need hemming around the edges, so it couldn't be easier!

Time Out for Jalapeños

Kristie Rigo
Friedens, PA

A different twist on the traditional deep-fried jalapeño poppers. My 16-year-old son Jared says these are the best!

8-oz. pkg. cream cheese, softened
2 c. shredded Cheddar cheese
1/2 lb. bacon, crisply cooked and crumbled

1/4 t. salt
1/4 t. chili powder
1/4 t. garlic powder
1 lb. jalapeños, halved
1/2 c. dry bread crumbs

Combine cheeses, bacon, salt and seasonings; fill each jalapeño half with mixture. Roll in bread crumbs; arrange on a greased baking sheet. Bake at 300 degrees for 30 to 35 minutes. Makes about 2 dozen.

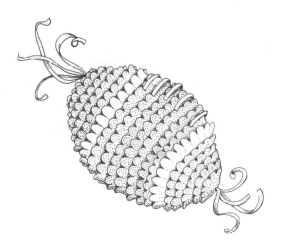

Make a football-shaped piñata...the kids will love it!

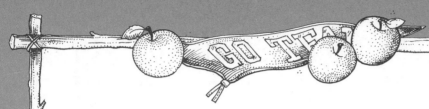

Super Sausage Bites

Sharon Cowan
Travis AFB, CA

I put this into a slow cooker to keep it warm until serving...nice for a tailgating party or neighborhood get-together.

1 lb. bacon, halved
2 1-lb. pkgs. Kielbasa, thickly
   sliced
8-oz. jar sweet-and-sour sauce

2 c. catsup
2 c. brown sugar, packed

Wrap one slice bacon around each piece of sausage; secure with a toothpick. Place in an ungreased 13"x9" baking pan; bake at 350 degrees for 30 minutes. Set aside. Mix remaining ingredients together; pour on top. Bake for one additional hour. Makes 2-1/2 dozen.

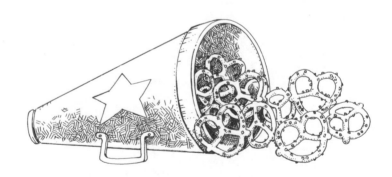

Giant megaphones are great for serving grab & go snacks like pretzels or chips. Just lay them on the buffet or picnic table and fill...a snap!

Quarterback-Sneak Squares

Anna Sherman
Poland, OH

No sneaking for these chicken appetizers...you'd better grab yours fast!

8-oz. pkg. cream cheese, softened
1/4 c. margarine, melted
1/2 t. salt
1 t. pepper
1/4 c. milk
2 T. green onions, chopped

4 c. chicken, cooked and shredded
2 8-oz. tubes refrigerated crescent rolls
10-3/4 oz. can cream of chicken soup
2/3 c. sour cream

Blend cream cheese, margarine, salt, pepper, milk and onion together; mix in chicken. Set aside. Unroll crescent rolls and form 8 squares by pinching 2 rolls together; spoon 1/2 cup chicken mixture onto each square. Fold up each corner; pinch sides together to form a pocket. Place on an ungreased baking sheet; bake at 325 degrees for 20 minutes or until golden. Set aside. Combine soup and sour cream in a saucepan; cook until heated through. Pour over squares before serving. Makes 8.

Show your spirit...dress up a garden scarecrow in a hometown football jersey!

Tailgate Party Sandwiches

Laurie Michael
Colorado Springs, CO

Easy to make and everyone always wants the recipe.

1 onion, chopped
1/2 c. margarine, softened
2 T. poppy seed
1 T. mustard
1 T. Worcestershire sauce

20 to 24 dinner rolls, halved
1 lb. baked ham, shaved
8-oz pkg. sliced Swiss cheese

Mix onion, margarine, poppy seed, mustard and Worcestershire sauce together; spread mixture on both sides of rolls. Cover one side with ham; place cheese over top. Replace top of roll; arrange on ungreased baking sheets. Bake at 400 degrees for 25 to 30 minutes or until cheese is melted; separate rolls before serving. Makes 20 to 24.

A neighborhood potluck is always a good idea to rally support before the "big game." Make it memorable...line picnic tables with placemats or table runners cut from green outdoor carpeting available at home improvement stores. Sure to make any table look like a football field!

Game-Winning Crab Spread

Trisha MacQueen
Bakersfield, CA

Garlic or rosemary bread is tasty dipped in this creamy spread.

8-oz. pkg. cream cheese, softened
1 c. mayonnaise
1 c. grated Parmesan cheese
6-oz. can flaked crabmeat

14-oz can artichoke hearts, drained
1/4 c. red pepper, chopped
1/4 c. green onion, chopped

Mix all ingredients together; spoon into a 13"x9" baking pan. Bake at 400 degrees for 20 minutes. Makes 5 to 6 cups.

Kids don't want to miss all the pre-game fun, so tote dinner along to enjoy at the stadium. Turn deflated footballs into serving plates by filling each with a sandwich, bag of chips and a couple of cookies…they'll be a hit.

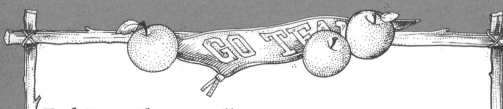

End-Zone Cheese Ball

Kristie Rigo
Friedens, PA

Best made several days ahead so the flavors can blend.
Serve with an assortment of crispy crackers.

8-oz. pkg. cream cheese,
   softened
1-1/2 t. horseradish
1/2 t. garlic salt

2-1/4 oz. jar dried chipped beef,
   chopped
3/4 c. chopped walnuts

Mix cream cheese, horseradish, garlic salt and dried beef together; shape into a ball. Roll in nuts; cover with plastic wrap and refrigerate for several hours before serving. Makes 10 servings.

Keep bottles of soda frosty in a metal pail sporting hometown colors...it's easy to make! Rub the pail with steel wool and add the team colors using enamel paint. Let dry overnight, then top with an acrylic spray sealer.

Undefeated Bacon-Cheese Dip

Kelly Hall
Butler, MO

You simply can't lose when you serve this cheesy dip!

1 lb. bacon, crisply cooked and crumbled
2 8-oz. pkgs. shredded Cheddar cheese
1/2 c. chopped pecans
2 c. mayonnaise-type salad dressing
1 onion, chopped

Mix all ingredients together. Serve with crackers. Makes about 7 cups.

Create a unique snack bowl in 5 minutes! Center an old record album on an upside-down, oven-safe bowl and place on a baking sheet. Watching carefully, bake at 300 degrees for 5 minutes. Remove the baking sheet from the oven and pull the record off the bowl and let cool. Remember these bowls aren't for hot foods or liquids, and should be lined with napkins before filling with snacks.

Championship Cheese Dip

Amanda Wells
Jemison, AL

Great with sturdy tortilla chip dippers!

1 lb. ground beef, browned
1 lb. ground sausage, browned
16-oz. pkg. pasteurized process
    cheese spread, cubed
8-oz. pkg. pasteurized process
    Mexican cheese spread,
    cubed

1 c. shredded Cheddar cheese
8-oz. jar salsa
1-1/4 oz. pkg. taco seasoning
    mix

Combine beef and sausage in a slow cooker; stir in remaining ingredients. Heat on high setting until cheeses are melted. Makes about 9 cups.

Score a touchdown with a tailgate decked out in hometown colors! Go to a local party supply store for pom-poms, strings of battery-operated lights and balloons, then give the kids football whistles and soft footballs to toss around during halftime.

Halftime Hoagie Dip

Linda Claus
Bensalem, PA

This spread goes great with Italian bread.

1/2 lb. sliced salami, chopped
1/2 lb. deli ham, chopped
1/2 lb. American cheese slices,
    chopped

3/4 c. tomato, chopped
1/3 c. onion, chopped
1/2 to 1 t. dried oregano
1/2 c. mayonnaise

Blend together all ingredients; chill. Makes about 7 cups.

Any hometown game can be a celebration! Make the evening
special…break out the sparklers!

Hand-Off Ham Ball

Faye LaRosa
McKeesport, PA

*I always serve this when friends are coming to
visit...everybody loves it!*

8-oz. cream cheese, softened
1/4 c. mayonnaise
2 c. cooked ham, ground
2 T. fresh parsley
1 t. onion, minced

1/2 t. dry mustard
1/4 t. Worcestershire sauce
Garnish: fresh parsley or nuts,
   chopped

Blend cream cheese and mayonnaise until smooth; stir in ham,
parsley, onion, mustard and Worcestershire sauce. Shape into 2 balls;
chill. Roll in nuts or parsley. Makes 2 balls.

A fireside cookout before or after a hometown football game
is a terrific idea on a chilly autumn night. Join the kids for a
friendly game of touch football, roasting hot dogs, making
s'mores and telling ghost stories...it's all about
making memories!

Running-Back Mushrooms

Brooke Sottosanti
Strongsville, OH

*Stuffed mushrooms so tasty, you'll find everyone
"running back" for more!*

8-oz. pkg. cream cheese,
    softened
1 bunch green onions, chopped
8 to 10 slices bacon, crisply
    cooked and crumbled

10 to 12 mushrooms, stems
    removed

Mix cream cheese, onions and bacon; spoon mixture into mushroom caps. Arrange on ungreased baking sheets; bake at 300 degrees for 10 to 20 minutes. Serves 8 to 10.

Clip newspaper articles about the football team's winning season, then decoupage them onto a vintage metal cooler. Toted to games & get-togethers, it's a great way to show hometown pride.

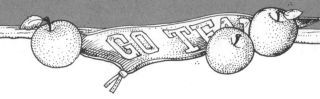

Swiss Mini Quiches

Irene Robinson
Cincinnati, OH

I make these ahead and freeze them, to be warmed up later in the oven. Great to have on hand for unexpected company.

1/2 c. plus 2 T. butter, softened
   and divided
3-oz. pkg. cream cheese,
   softened
1 c. all-purpose flour
1/2 lb. mushrooms, diced

1 onion, diced
1 c. shredded Swiss cheese
1/2 c. bacon bits
1 egg, slightly beaten
1/2 c. milk
1/4 t. salt

Cream together 1/2 cup butter and cream cheese; blend in flour. Roll into 24 balls and press into greased mini muffin cups. Melt remaining butter in skillet; heat mushrooms and onions until softened. Spoon mixture into muffin cups; sprinkle with cheese and bacon bits. Blend together egg, milk and salt; spoon into muffin cups. Bake at 350 degrees for 30 minutes until golden. Makes 2 dozen.

Make it easy for the kids to find where all the yummy halftime snacks are...tie a team banner or flag to the car antenna!

It's a Snap Sourdough Dip

Michele Richards
Reading, PA

A snap to make...what else can we say?

8-oz. pkg. shredded Cheddar
   cheese
8-oz. pkg. shredded mozzarella
   cheese

1 onion, diced
2 c. mayonnaise
1/2 t. Worcestershire sauce
1 loaf sourdough bread

Mix together cheeses, onion, mayonnaise and Worcestershire sauce; set aside. Cut the center out of the bread; tear into bite-size pieces. Spoon cheese mixture into the center of the bread; bake at 350 degrees for 30 minutes or until cheese is bubbling. Serve with sourdough bread. Makes 6 cups.

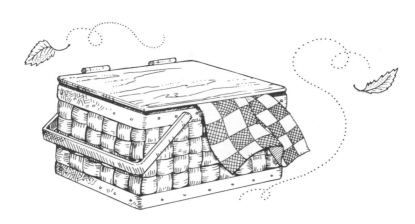

If game night weather turns rainy, it's still easy to have family tailgating fun...lift up the tailgate, spread a stadium blanket or checkered tablecloth in the back and enjoy pregame munchies picnic style!

43

3-Cheers Caramel Dip

Jenifer Crane
Katy, TX

Worth cheering for!

8-oz. pkg. cream cheese,
  softened
1 c. brown sugar, packed
1/2 t. vanilla extract

1/2 t. cinnamon
8-oz. container frozen whipped
  topping, thawed

Blend all ingredients together. Serve with assorted fruit. Makes about 5 cups.

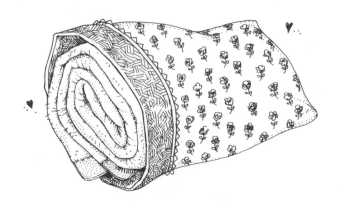

Slip a cozy fleece blanket into a pillowcase…the blanket keeps kids toasty during the game, and tucked back inside the pillowcase, it becomes a handy pillow for little ones to nap on during the drive home.

44

Hometown Football Frenzy

Winning Pumpkin Dip

Peg Ackerman
Pasadena, CA

This creamy dip will be a winner even during overtime!

29-oz. can pumpkin pie filling
4 c. powdered sugar
2 8-oz. pkgs. cream cheese,
   softened

2 t. cinnamon
1 t. ground ginger
gingersnap cookies

Combine pumpkin, sugar and cream cheese in a serving bowl. Mix well; stir in cinnamon and ginger. Arrange bowl on a plate; surround with gingersnaps. Makes 7 cups.

Homecoming games are a big community event!
Keep all those memories by placing game tickets, newspaper articles, pennants and favorite photos in a combination of frames and shadow boxes.

Goal-Line Caramel Corn

Tonya Sheppard
Galveston, TX

The perfect combination of gingerbread and caramel corn flavors.

15 c. popped popcorn
1/2 t. salt
1 c. butter
2 c. brown sugar, packed
1/4 c. corn syrup

1/4 c. molasses
1 T. ground ginger
1 t. cinnamon
1/2 t. baking soda

Divide popcorn equally between two lightly greased 13"x9" baking pans; set aside. Combine salt, butter, brown sugar, corn syrup, molasses, ginger and cinnamon in a large, heavy saucepan. Heat over medium heat until mixture boils. Boil for 5 minutes; stirring frequently. Remove from heat; add baking soda. Pour over popcorn; toss to coat. Bake at 250 degrees for one hour, stirring every 15 minutes until popcorn is crisp. Cool completely; store in airtight containers. Makes 15 servings.

Score big with football-shaped invitations cut from corrugated cardboard. Jot the party information on the back, then, on the front, tie on a white shoelace slipped through holes made with a hole punch, for the football lacing. Fun!

46

Red Hot Cinnamon Popcorn

Lorie McGuire
Erie, KS

Makes so much, have a scoop and lunch-size brown paper bags on hand so guests can serve themselves.

1 c. butter
1/2 c. corn syrup
1/2 t. salt

8-oz. pkg. red cinnamon candies
32 c. popped popcorn

Place butter, syrup, salt and candies in a heavy saucepan. Bring to a boil over medium heat and boil for 5 minutes; stir constantly. Pour over popcorn; mix until well coated. Spread popcorn on a greased aluminum foil-lined baking sheet; bake at 250 degrees for 15 minutes. Cool; store in an airtight container. Makes 32 servings.

I am delighted to have you play football.
I believe in rough, manly sports.

-Theodore Roosevelt

Sugary Cinnamon Walnuts

Pat Certisimo
Evans, GA

These never fail to get compliments and recipe requests!

1 egg white
1 t. water
1-lb. pkg. walnuts

1 c. sugar
2-1/4 t. cinnamon
1 t. salt

Beat egg white with water until stiff peaks form; fold in walnuts. Set aside. Mix together sugar, cinnamon and salt; add to walnut mixture, blending completely. Spread on a greased baking sheet; bake at 250 degrees for one hour, stirring every 15 minutes. Makes one pound.

Harvest Trail Mix

Irene Whatling
West Des Moines, IA

Use Valentine or Christmas colored candy-coated chocolates and you have a snack that's colorful, as well as tasty, year 'round.

10.5-oz. box bite-size crispy
   honey nut corn & rice cereal
   squares
8-oz. pkg. candy-coated chocolates

8-oz. bag candy corn
9-oz. pkg. raisins
12-oz. jar dry-roasted peanuts

Mix all ingredients together; store in an airtight container. Makes 3 pounds.

Buttery Pecan Bars

Gladys Kielar
Perrysburg, OH

*My husband's family hosts an outdoor reunion each Labor Day
and this dessert is always on the menu.*

3 c. all-purpose flour
2 c. sugar, divided
1 c. butter
1/2 t. salt
4 eggs, beaten

1-1/2 c. corn syrup
3 T. butter, melted
1-1/2 t. vanilla extract
2-1/2 c. chopped pecans

Mix flour, 1/2 cup sugar. butter and salt together until mixture
resembles crumbs; set aside. Press into a well-greased jelly-roll pan;
bake at 350 degrees for 15 minutes. Combine eggs, corn syrup, melted
butter, vanilla, pecans and remaining sugar until well blended; pour
over hot crust. Return to oven for 25 additional minutes; cool and cut
into bars. Makes 25.

Keep the hometown game fun for little ones
too…toss crushed ice and juice boxes into
upside-down football helmets.

Sweet & Spicy Pumpkin Seeds

Angie Venable
Gooseberry Patch

My kids love these...they can hardly wait for them to cool!

1 c. pumpkin seeds
5 T. sugar, divided
1/4 t. salt
1/4 t. dried cumin

1/4 t. cinnamon
1/4 t. ground ginger
1/8 t. cayenne pepper
1-1/2 T. peanut oil

Lay pumpkin seeds on a baking sheet lined with wax paper; bake at 250 degrees for one hour or until dry. Cool. In a bowl, combine 3 tablespoons sugar, salt, cumin, cinnamon, ginger and pepper; set aside. Heat oil in a skillet; add pumpkin seeds and remaining sugar. Cook for 45 minutes or until sugar melts and pumpkin seeds begin to caramelize. Transfer to a bowl; stir to coat. Cool. Makes about one cup.

The woods are full of fairies;
The sea is full of fish;
The trees are full of golden leaves;
Let's make an autumn wish.

-Unknown

AUCTIONS & BARN Sales

Hot Caramel Apple Cider

Sharon Demers
Dolores, CO

*This warm, spiced cider couldn't be easier to make and
the aroma and taste are wonderful.*

1 gal. apple cider
1 pkg. mulling spices
12-oz. jar caramel ice cream
    topping
1 c. whipping cream

2 to 3 t. sugar
1/2 t. vanilla extract
Garnish: cinnamon sticks,
    ground cinnamon

Heat cider and mulling spices as directed on spice package. When
thoroughly heated, pour into individual cups and top with one
teaspoon caramel topping; stir to dissolve. Place whipping cream and
sugar in a bowl; add vanilla. Using an electric mixer, blend until soft
peaks form. Add a dollop to each mug of cider; garnish with a
cinnamon stick and a sprinkle of cinnamon. Makes about 32 servings.

Autumn auctions start early so pulling together an auction
"kit" the night before will make sure you don't miss out on
any of the bargains! Fill a backpack with an antique
guidebook, map, extra sweater, tape measure and some trail
mix for snacking…it's bound to be a fun day!

Maple Nut Bread

Renae Scheiderer
Beallsville, OH

Top thick slices with creamery butter...delicious!

2 c. all-purpose flour
4 t. baking powder
1 t. salt
3/4 c. milk

1/4 c. maple syrup
1 egg, beaten
1 c. chopped nuts or raisins

Stir flour, baking powder and salt together. Blend in milk, syrup and egg. Add nuts or raisins, mixing well. Pour into a greased 9"x5" loaf pan; bake at 350 degrees for one hour. Serves 8.

The prettiest linens can often be found at bargain prices during a busy auction. Even if they're slightly worn, beautiful handmade napkins and pillowcases can easily be turned into one-of-a-kind pillow covers, table runners or cafe curtains.

Molasses Sugar Cookies

Denise Mainville
Elk Rapids, MI

Fifteen years ago after finishing my day's work, I arrived at the home of my daughter's babysitter and walked into the most wonderful aroma of my favorite cookie...this recipe is the best!

1-1/2 c. brown sugar, packed
3/4 c. margarine
2 eggs
3 T. molasses
2 t. baking soda
1/2 t. ground ginger

1/2 t. ground cloves
1 t. cinnamon
1/2 t. salt
2-1/2 c. all-purpose flour
Garnish: sugar

Combine brown sugar, margarine, eggs and molasses; blend well. Stir in remaining ingredients and refrigerate dough for one hour. Form dough into one-inch balls and roll into sugar. Arrange 2 inches apart on ungreased baking sheets at 350 degrees for 8 to 10 minutes. Makes 4 to 5 dozen.

Be on the lookout for cobalt and amber bottles at barn sales. They can be found in all shapes and sizes and are still very affordable! Filled with just-picked flowers, they're charming sitting on a windowsill where they'll reflect the sunlight.

Hot Berry Cider

Delinda Blakney
Dallas, GA

A mug will warm you head to toe.

1 gal. apple cider
32-oz. bottle cranberry juice
  cocktail

8 allspice berries
8 whole cloves
2 cinnamon sticks, halved

Combine all ingredients; bring to a boil. Reduce heat and simmer for 30 minutes. Strain to remove spices; serve. Makes 20 servings.

Cranberry Tea

Della Feist
Faith, SD

This is a favorite drink around our home during the fall and winter holidays. I make a double batch and invite friends.

16-oz. bag frozen cranberries,
  thawed
1 cinnamon stick
2 qts. water
6-oz. can frozen orange juice
  concentrate, thawed

6-oz. can frozen lemonade
  concentrate, thawed
1 c. sugar

Boil cranberries and cinnamon stick in water for 5 minutes; strain. Add concentrates and sugar; blend well. Serve warm. Makes 20 servings.

Apple Baked Beans

Tina Wright
Atlanta, GA

*Search flea markets and antique shops for an old-fashioned
bean pot...ideal for baking this recipe in.*

1/4 c. butter
3 c. Granny Smith apples, peeled
   and cubed
1/2 c. brown sugar, packed
1/4 c. sugar

48-oz. jar Great Northern beans
1/2 c. catsup
1 t. cinnamon
1 T. molasses
Optional: 1 t. salt

Melt butter in a saucepan; add apples and heat until tender. Add
sugars; continue heating until sugars are dissolved. Stir in remaining
ingredients; pour into a greased 2-quart casserole dish. Bake for one
hour at 350 degrees. Makes 6 to 8 servings.

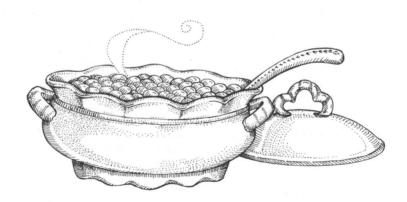

Don't pass up an ironstone treasure just because it's yellowed
with age...soak dishes in hydrogen peroxide to help bring
back the original white color.

Sloppy Joes

Ruth Ann Maynard
Nixa, MO

Pick up colorful bandannas whenever you spot them at sales...ideal lap-size napkins for these sloppy, Sloppy Joes!

1 lb. ground beef
1/2 c. onion, chopped
1/4 c. green pepper, chopped
1/4 c. celery, chopped
10-3/4 oz. can tomato soup

1/4 c. catsup
1 T. vinegar
1 T. sugar
1/8 t. pepper
1 t. salt

Combine beef with onion, green pepper and celery in a skillet; heat until beef is browned. Mix in remaining ingredients; lower heat and simmer for 20 minutes. Makes 6 servings.

The rich color of vintage copper shines in the Fall. Strainers, pots, molds and trays are not only practical, but filled with mums, dahlias, yarrow or bittersweet, they make decorating a snap!

Sweet Potato Salad

Ginger Konerman
Turtletown, TN

A recipe my family loves...truly a family favorite!

3 lbs. sweet potatoes, peeled,
    cubed and boiled
6 green onions, chopped

5 stalks celery, chopped
1-1/2 c. mayonnaise
2 T. Dijon mustard

Place potatoes, onion and celery in a bowl; set aside. Combine mayonnaise and mustard; stir into potato mixture. Chill. Makes 6 to 8 servings.

Salvage trim pieces like spindles make incredible photo frames. Trim 2 spindles to any size for the frame sides, then have 2 pieces of glass cut to fit. Slip a photo between the glass, set between the spindles and attach trim pieces to the top and bottom with nails to secure. A great look!

Delicious BBQ Hamburgers

Dee Ann Ice
Delaware, OH

*Go ahead and double the recipe, then freeze half for a
ready-made dinner another day.*

1 lb. ground beef
1/2 c. milk
1/2 c. bread crumbs
1/4 t. pepper
1/4 t. garlic powder
1/2 c. onion, chopped

1/2 c. green pepper, chopped
1 c. catsup
2 t. vinegar
2 t. mustard
1/2 c. sugar
3/4 t. salt

Combine beef, milk, bread crumbs, pepper, garlic powder, onion and
green pepper; mix well. Shape into patties and place in a skillet; brown
both sides. Place in a greased 13"x9" baking pan; set aside. Combine
remaining ingredients in a mixing bowl; pour over patties. Bake at
350 degrees for one hour. Serves 4 to 6.

Surround an old-fashioned slate chalkboard with bunches of
colorful fall berries or preserved oak leaves. Hanging on a
door, it's a whimsical place to jot down seasonal
greetings for visitors.

Ultimate Chicken Salad Sandwiches

John Grashoff
Fort Wayne, IN

I always remember Grandma when I make these sandwiches...one of her special meals whenever I came to visit.

8-oz. can white chicken breast
1 to 2 c. mayonnaise
1 to 2 c. celery, chopped

1 to 2 T. sweet relish
salt and pepper to taste
1 loaf sliced oatmeal bread

Mix first 4 ingredients together; sprinkle with salt and pepper. Spread on bread. Serves 4 to 6.

Auctions can turn up lots of trunks that have roomy drawers or cubbies inside. What terrific storage for any room when filled with books, videos, games or blankets.

Honey Quick Bread

Flo Burtnett
Gage, OK

Homemade bread in almost no time!

2-1/2 c. all-purpose flour	1/4 t. cinnamon
1 t. baking soda	1/2 c. oil
1/2 t. salt	1-1/2 c. buttermilk
1 t. baking powder	1/2 c. honey

Mix all ingredients together; spoon into a greased and floured
9"x5" loaf pan. Let stand for 20 minutes; then bake at 375 degrees for
50 to 60 minutes. Makes one loaf.

A vintage tea tray topped with a quilt square or colorful
handkerchief makes breakfast in bed a cozy idea!

Italian Pork Sandwiches

Darla Kerns
Rittman, OH

A savory slow-cooker meal.

2 lbs. ground pork, browned
8-oz. can tomato sauce
15-oz. can pizza sauce
1 T. Worcestershire sauce
1-1/2 cloves garlic, chopped
2 T. vinegar

1 t. salt
1/2 t. fennel seed
hot pepper sauce to taste
sandwich buns, split
Garnish: shredded mozzarella
    cheese

Place pork in a slow cooker; stir in sauces and seasonings. Cover and cook on low setting for 8 to 10 hours. Spoon onto buns; top with shredded cheese. Makes about 8 servings.

Slow cookers are great for cooking meals while you're barn sale-ing...come home to a meal ready to enjoy!

Hot Chicken Salad

Annette Ingram
Grand Rapids, MI

Try topping with crushed potato chips before baking...adds extra crunch!

2 c. cooked chicken breast, diced
2 c. celery, diced
8-oz. can sliced water chestnuts, drained
1/2 c. chopped pecans

1 c. mayonnaise
1/2 t. celery salt
2 T. lemon juice
2 t. onion, minced
1/2 c. shredded Swiss cheese

Mix together all ingredients except Swiss cheese and potato chips. Spread in a lightly greased 8"x8" baking dish. Sprinkle with shredded cheese. Bake at 350 degrees for 15 to 20 minutes or until heated through. Makes 4 to 6 servings.

You can find some beautiful, big stoneware casserole dishes at auctions...nice and roomy enough for a family-size recipe.

Auction Chili

Sandi Boothman
Camden, MI

Our church ladies' mission group has an auction every year and we make this chili for the youth group to sell as a fundraiser. We always get compliments from the auctioneers that it is the best chili they have ever tasted!

1 lb. ground beef
1 onion, chopped
1 t. oil
15-oz. can diced tomatoes
10-3/4 oz. can tomato soup
15-oz. can kidney beans,
    drained

salt to taste
1/8 t. pepper
1/4 t. dried cumin
1/2 t. chili powder

Brown ground beef and onion together in oil; drain. Add remaining ingredients; heat until warmed through. Makes 4 to 6 servings.

Why not bring an Adirondack chair indoors?
It's great for giving a carefree country feeling to any room!

Spicy Cornbread

Monarie Carraro
Bigelow, AR

Nothing goes with chili like cornbread...try this hot version for a change of pace.

2 8-1/2 oz. pkgs. corn muffin
   mix
2 T. oil
4 jalapeño peppers, chopped

1/2 c. corn
1/4 c. sour cream
2 T. honey

Prepare muffin mix according to package directions; stir in remaining ingredients. Pour into a greased 13"x9" baking dish; bake for 18 to 20 minutes at 400 degrees or until golden. Makes 9 to 12 servings.

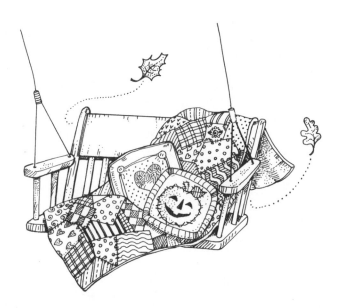

Create the perfect porch with auction finds. Nothing says "country" like a porch swing, vintage chairs, birdhouses and a wooden glider. How relaxing!

Bean, Bacon & Potato Soup

Ed Kielar
Perrrysburg, OH

My mother, who made sure all 4 sons learned to cook, shared this recipe with me. Chilly weekends at home are ideal for enjoying this warming soup...and to remember cooking with Mom.

6 to 8 slices bacon, crisply
   cooked and crumbled,
   drippings reserved
1/3 c. green pepper, chopped
1 onion, chopped
5 T. all-purpose flour, divided
2 qts. water

3 c. green beans, chopped
2 c. potatoes, peeled and diced
2 sprigs fresh dill, chopped
1/2 t. celery seed
salt and pepper to taste
1/2 c. sour cream

Place reserved drippings in a skillet; heat green pepper and onion until onion is golden. Stir in 3 tablespoons flour; heat until golden. Add all remaining ingredients except sour cream and remaining 2 tablespoons flour; bring to a boil. Reduce heat and simmer, covered, 45 minutes to one hour. Blend remaining flour with sour cream. Stir 1/4 cup hot soup broth into sour cream mixture, mixing well. Stir mixture into soup; add bacon. Reduce heat and simmer 5 minutes. Let stand 10 minutes before serving. Makes about 10 servings.

A wire jar lifter, found inside water bath canners, makes a pretty flower holder when filled with canning jars and handpicked bouquets.

Hearty Stuffed Hamburgers

Malacha Payton
Edmond, OK

You can serve on buns, but there's no need to...these are a meal all by themselves!

1 lb. ground beef	1 onion, grated
1/2 t. salt	1/2 c. dry bread cubes
1/4 t. pepper	4 slices onion
1/2 t. dried sage	4 slices tomato
1/4 c. milk	dill pickle slices to taste

Combine ground beef, salt, pepper, sage, milk, grated onion and bread cubes, mixing well. Shape into 8 patties. On each of 4 patties, place one slice onion, one slice tomato and dill pickles, topping each with a remaining patty. Crimp edges to seal. Place on a broiler pan; broil 6 minutes. Turn and broil an additional 6 minutes. Makes 4 servings.

Be creative...fill cast iron or stone urns with more than just flowers, top each with a plump pumpkin. What a terrific addition for any front porch!

Slow-Cooker BBQ Beef

Cynthia Babish
Carnegie, PA

For an auction tailgate picnic, spoon Slow-Cooker BBQ Beef over buns and wrap in aluminum foil. Tuck a bag of chips and some juice boxes in a picnic basket and you're all set!

4-lb. beef chuck roast
2 stalks celery, chopped
1 green pepper, chopped
1 onion, chopped
14-oz. bottle catsup

3 T. vinegar
1 T. hot pepper sauce
1 T. pepper
1-1/2 c. water

Cut roast into 4 sections; place in a slow cooker. Add celery, green pepper and onion. Mix together catsup, vinegar, hot pepper sauce, pepper and water in a small mixing bowl; pour over beef mixture. Cook on high setting for 4 to 6 hours or until meat is very tender. Shred to serve. Serves 8.

Barn sales turn up all kinds of fun possibilities!
The nooks in an old dollhouse can hold bathroom
necessities, while a doll bed on wheels
can double as a laundry room hamper.

Fresh Tomato Pie

Grace Woodruff
Pine Bluff, AR

If your family loves tomatoes, you'll want to make more than one of these...it's like a grown-up version of a tomato sandwich!

1 c. mayonnaise
1 c. grated Parmesan cheese
3 to 4 tomatoes, peeled and
    sliced
9-inch deep-dish pie crust,
    baked

6 to 8 slices bacon, crisply
    cooked and crumbled
salt and pepper to taste

Blend mayonnaise and Parmesan cheese together; set aside. Layer half the tomatoes into the pie crust, sprinkle with bacon. Add remaining tomatoes; salt and pepper to taste. Spread mayonnaise mixture on top, spreading to edges. Bake at 400 degrees for 15 to 17 minutes, or until top is lightly golden. Makes 8 servings.

Be creative and let auction treasures replace more modern items...a sturdy farmhouse table makes a handy kitchen island while a porcelain-topped table makes a great office desk.

Velvety Smooth Pumpkin Soup

Mary Murray
Gooseberry Patch

Pour this creamy pumpkin soup into a thermos and tote along to auctions and barn sales. It will warm you head to toe!

1/4 c. butter
1 onion, chopped
1 T. brown sugar, packed
14.5-oz. can chicken broth
1/2 c. water

15-oz. can pumpkin
12-oz. can evaporated milk
1 t. garlic salt
1/4 t. cinnamon
salt and pepper to taste

Melt butter in a saucepan over medium heat. Add onion and brown sugar; cook until onion is transparent. Add broth and water; bring to a boil. Reduce heat to a simmer and stir in remaining ingredients; blend well. Simmer until soup is heated through; do not allow to boil. Makes 6 servings.

Snap up decorative muffin tins…ideal for organizing desk supplies like push pins, paper clips and rubber bands.

Turkey-Veggie Bagels

April Jacobs
Loveland, CO

Instead of bagels, you can also slice a loaf of round bread in half and layer on all the goodies. Replace the top of the loaf, cut into wedges and secure the sandwich in plastic wrap...an easy take-along lunch.

4 onion bagels, sliced in half
4 leaves Romaine lettuce
8 slices smoked deli turkey
1 cucumber, sliced thin

2 to 4 radishes, thinly sliced
1/4 c. cream cheese with chives
   and onions
1 to 2 carrots, shredded

Arrange 4 bagel halves on serving tray. Place a lettuce leaf on each; top with turkey, cucumber, radish and carrot. Spread cream cheese on top halves of bagels; place on bottom halves. Makes 4.

Look at auction finds in new ways...turn an architectural star into an office paperweight, hang an old-fashioned grater upside-down on the wall and use the handle as a dish towel holder or create a clutter catcher from a metal chicken nester.

Apple-Walnut Ring Cake

Jeanna Vinai
Wildwood, MO

I love this dessert...it's one of the main reasons I go apple picking!

1 c. shortening, softened
2 c. sugar
3 eggs
3 c. all-purpose flour
1-1/2 t. baking soda
1/2 t. salt

1 t. cinnamon
1/4 t. mace
2 t. vanilla extract
3 c. apples, cored, peeled and
    chopped
2 c. chopped walnuts

Cream shortening and sugar together until fluffy. Add eggs, one at a time, beating well after each addition; set aside. Mix and sift flour, baking soda, salt, cinnamon and mace; add gradually to mixture. Stir in vanilla, apples and nuts; spoon into greased and floured 10" tube pan. Bake at 325 degrees for 1-1/2 hours. Let cool in pan for 10 minutes. Remove from pan to wire rack to cool completely. Makes 8 to 10 servings.

INDIAN SUMMER
Potluck

Fall Delight

Shaney Smith
Gilbert, AZ

This tasty dinner-in-a-pumpkin will be a hit at any gathering!

1 onion, chopped
2 T. oil
2 lbs. ground beef
2 T. soy sauce
2 T. brown sugar, packed
4-oz. can sliced mushrooms,
   drained

10-3/4 oz. can cream of chicken
   soup
1-1/2 c. prepared white rice
8-oz. can sliced water chestnuts,
   drained
1 pumpkin, seeded

Sauté onion in oil; add beef. Cook until browned; stir in soy sauce, brown sugar, mushrooms and soup. Simmer for 10 minutes; add rice and water chestnuts. Mix well; set aside. Place pumpkin on a greased baking sheet; spoon beef mixture inside pumpkin. Replace top; bake at 350 degrees for one hour. Serves 6 to 8.

If the weather's beautiful, consider hosting a
potluck dinner outside in all of autumn's glory! Set up a
farm table scattered with leaves and a wheat-filled
sap bucket centerpiece...celebrate!

Homestyle Macaroni & Cheese

Sharon Crider
St. Robert, MO

Isn't this every little one's favorite dish? A can't-miss recipe.

2 c. prepared elbow macaroni
1/4 c. butter
1/4 c. all-purpose flour
2-1/4 c. milk

1/4 c. onion, minced
1/2 t. salt
2 c. shredded Cheddar cheese
2 c. cooked ham, diced

Place prepared macaroni in an ungreased 2-quart casserole dish. Melt butter in a saucepan over medium heat; add flour and cook slowly, stirring until bubbly. Add milk, onion and salt; stir until slightly thickened. Blend in cheese; stir until melted. Add ham to macaroni; stir in cheese mixture. Bake at 350 degrees for 20 to 25 minutes; let stand 5 minutes before serving. Makes 4 to 6 servings.

Everyone must take time to sit
and watch the leaves turn.

-Elizabeth Lawrence

Ham with Orange-Mustard Glaze

Tiffany Brinkley
Broomfield, CO

A delicious ham for a crowd.

6 to 8-lb. fully cooked bone-in
   ham half
1 c. water
1 c. dry sherry or orange juice

2/3 c. orange marmalade
1/3 c. stone-ground mustard
1 T. dry mustard

Place ham, fat-side up, on a rack in a shallow roasting pan. Pour water into pan; bake for one hour at 325 degrees. Remove from oven; add sherry or orange juice to pan. Trim fat from ham as necessary. Score ham diagonally at one-inch intervals, cutting about 1/4 inch deep; score in opposite direction to form diamond shapes. Insert meat thermometer so bulb reaches center of thickest part of ham but does not rest in fat or on bone. Combine marmalade and mustards in a small bowl; mix well and brush half of mixture over ham. Baste ham with pan juices; return to oven. Bake an additional one hour to 90 minutes, or until meat thermometer registers 140 degrees; baste frequently with pan juices and brush with remaining marmalade mixture. Allow ham to stand in roasting pan for 15 minutes before slicing, basting frequently with pan juices. Serve warm or cold. Makes 16 servings.

Tote potluck necessities in a wheeled basket...so easy! Vintage rolling totes can be found at shows and shops, or check out wicker stores for brand-new ones.

Superb Squash

Wendy Lee Paffenroth
Pine Island, NY

Even those who say they don't like squash will love this...just don't tell them what's in it until they've tried it!

3/4 lb. zucchini, sliced
3/4 lb. yellow squash, sliced
1/2 c. butter, melted and divided
1 to 2 c. herbed stuffing mix, divided
10-3/4 oz. can cream of chicken soup

1 c. sour cream
2-oz. jar pimentos, sliced and drained
8-oz. can water chestnuts, drained
2 onions, chopped

Place zucchini and yellow squash in a saucepan; cover with water. Cook until tender, about 5 minutes; drain and set aside. Melt 1/4 cup butter in saucepan; stir in half the stuffing mix. Spread into the bottom of a lightly greased 2-quart casserole dish; set aside. Add soup, sour cream, pimentos, water chestnuts and onions to zucchini mixture; mix well. Spread over stuffing mixture; set aside. In another bowl, stir remaining butter into remaining stuffing mix. Spoon onto squash mixture; bake at 350 degrees for 30 minutes. Serves 4 to 6.

Looking for a spectacular centerpiece? Look no more! Arrange brightly colored fall leaves such as sumac, aspen and maple with bunches of winterberries and sedum. Tucked inside a white Lumina pumpkin and set atop a cake plate, it's beautiful!

Potluck Pork Chops

Tina Vogel
Tampa, FL

We like these tender pork chops served alongside rice or egg noodles.

6 pork chops
2 T. oil
1 tomato, chopped
1 onion, chopped
1 green pepper, chopped
1 c. sliced mushrooms
salt and pepper to taste

2 t. dried basil
garlic powder to taste
10 3/4-oz. can tomato soup
1/4 c. white wine or chicken
   broth
1/4 c. sour cream
2/3 c. water

Brown pork chops in oil over medium-high heat; set aside, reserving drippings in skillet. Cook tomato, onion, green pepper and mushrooms in same skillet; stir in salt, pepper, basil and garlic powder. Add tomato soup, wine or broth and sour cream; blend in water. Place pork chops back into skillet and simmer, covered, for 15 to 20 minutes over medium heat. Makes 6 servings.

Lined with a tea towel, vintage cherry-picking pails make
handy potluck take-alongs for rolls, fresh
fruit, napkins and silverware.

Potato Quiche

Ruth Ahders
Schenectady, NY

For variety, I sometimes add ham or spinach to taste with the egg and cheese mixture...try adding your favorite combinations!

16-oz. bag frozen hashbrowns
2 T. oil
1 onion, chopped

4 to 5 eggs, beaten
1 c. shredded Cheddar cheese

In a large skillet, fry hashbrowns and onion in oil until golden. Press potato mixture into a greased 9" deep-dish glass pie plate. Blend eggs with cheese and pour into crust. Bake at 350 degrees for 35 minutes until set. Makes 8 servings.

Keep beverages warm and always have a napkin handy...wrap them together! Just wrap a napkin around a mug and secure a napkin ring. Fill the mug with any favorite spiced cider or cocoa...quick & easy!

Chicken & Dumplings

Kathy Uhruh
Fresno, CA

There's nothing like this for comfort food.

3 lbs. skinless, boneless chicken
1 onion, chopped
2 carrots, chopped
3 stalks celery, chopped
3 cloves garlic, minced
2 bay leaves
1 t. dried thyme

4 sprigs fresh parsley
1-1/2 t. salt
1/2 t. pepper
1 c. all-purpose flour
2 t. baking powder
1/2 c. milk
Garnish: fresh parsley sprigs

Place chicken in a Dutch oven with onion, carrots, celery, garlic, bay leaves, thyme and parsley. Sprinkle with salt and pepper; add enough water to cover chicken. Bring just to a boil over medium-high heat; reduce heat to low and simmer, covered, until chicken is tender, about one hour. Remove chicken and set aside until cool enough to handle, then cut into bite-size pieces. Remove bay leaves from broth and discard; heat broth to a slow boil. Combine flour, baking powder and remaining salt in a medium mixing bowl; stir in milk and beat until stiff. Drop batter, one tablespoon at a time, into the boiling broth. Cover and cook for 10 minutes. Add reserved chicken and cook until heated through, about 5 minutes. The dumplings should be puffed and the meat warmed through. Garnish with additional parsley. Serves 8.

If a Fall potluck is outdoors, wrap leaves around glass votive candle holders and secure with cotton string. Marching them down the center of the table adds such pretty flickering light.

Aunt Mary's Cornbread Salad

Barbara Lewis
Auburn, CA

An old-fashioned recipe that's worth remembering.

4 c. cornbread, crumbled
2 c. chicken, cooked and
  chopped
1 c. green onion, chopped
1 c. fresh parsley, chopped
1/2 c. green pepper, chopped
1/2 c. dill pickles, chopped
1/2 c. sliced water chestnuts
1 T. diced pimento
15-1/4 oz. can peas, drained

15-oz. can shoepeg corn,
  drained
1-1/2 T. sugar
1 t. salt
1/2 t. pepper
1 t. poultry seasoning
1/4 t. cayenne pepper
1 c. mayonnaise
Garnish: paprika

Mix together all ingredients except paprika in a serving bowl, stirring in mayonnaise last. Cover and chill for several hours. Sprinkle with paprika before serving. Serves 12 to 15.

Looking for a fun placecard idea? Tuck a napkin and silverware inside a tall glass. Jot names down on mailing tags, slip string through the tag holes and tie one around each set of silverware.

Cinnamon Chicken

Jennifer Eveland-Kupp
Temple, PA

I think this recipe is so delicious, it's sure to please any family.

1/2 c. sherry or chicken broth
2 t. cinnamon
1/3 c. honey
2 T. lemon juice

1/2 t. curry powder
1 t. garlic salt
2 whole chickens, cut up

Blend together sherry or broth, cinnamon, honey, lemon juice, curry powder and garlic salt. Arrange chicken pieces in a large ungreased roasting pan; pour mixture over chicken. Cover and refrigerate several hours or overnight. Bake at 375 degrees for one hour or until juices run clear when chicken is pierced. Makes 12 to 16 servings.

Send potluck invitations that are ready in no time. Purchase kraft-paper tags, they already have the rich color and feel of Fall, then add typewriter-key stickers for all the get-together details!

Crunchy Appleslaw

Jo Ann

Try mixing up the taste of this slaw by substituting ground ginger and pecans or ground cumin and cashews for the Italian seasoning and walnuts.

3 apples, cored and thinly sliced
2 green onions, chopped
2 stalks celery, chopped
1/2 c. carrots, grated
1/2 c. cabbage, grated

1/2 c. zucchini, grated
1 c. mayonnaise
1 to 2 t. Italian seasoning
1/2 c. chopped walnuts, toasted

Combine apples, onions, celery, carrots, cabbage and zucchini in a serving bowl; set aside. Whisk mayonnaise with Italian seasoning and walnuts in a small bowl; gently toss with apple mixture until coated. Cover and refrigerate 3 to 4 hours to allow flavors to blend. Makes 6 to 8 servings.

Items gathered on a quick trip to the local farm stand mean a bounty of ideas for greeting family & friends. Porch columns are so pretty wrapped with bittersweet vines, then just top off the railing with a row of birdhouse gourds…done!

Baked Chicken Salad

Lisa Ludwig
Fort Wayne, IN

So versatile, you can use any cheese, substitute green olives for black, and use red onion for more color...you can't go wrong.

3 c. cooked chicken, diced
1 c. celery, sliced
1 c. shredded sharp Cheddar
   cheese, divided
1/4 c. black olives, chopped
1 T. onion, minced

1 t. salt
mayonnaise-type salad dressing
   to taste
1 c. potato chips, crushed

Combine chicken, celery, 1/2 cup cheese, olives, onion and salt; add enough salad dressing to moisten. Place in a well-greased 13"x9" baking pan; top with potato chips and remaining cheese. Bake at 350 degrees for 30 minutes. Serves 4.

Head to the great outdoors for a family potluck! Toss lots of colorful blankets and quilts on the tables and then after lunch, play games or take a nature hike while the leaves are at their prettiest.

Indian Summer Potluck

Jill's Corn Cakes & Salsa

Linda Reynolds
Cut Bank, MT

Jicama, also known as a Mexican potato, is a large vegetable easily found in most grocery stores. If you've never tried them, you really should…they give the salsa recipe a nice crunch.

1 T. butter, melted
16-oz. pkg. frozen corn, thawed
1 egg
1/3 c. red pepper, diced
1/3 c. milk

3 T. cornmeal
1/3 c. all-purpose flour
1-1/2 t. sugar
1-1/2 t. baking powder

In a bowl, combine butter, corn, egg, red pepper and milk; set aside. In a separate bowl, mix cornmeal, flour, sugar and baking powder; add to corn mixture. Mix well and form into 6 patties. Over medium heat, cook patties in a saucepan lightly coated with non-stick cooking spray. Continue to cook and turn until patties are golden on both sides. Serve with Black Bean Salsa. Serves 6.

Black Bean Salsa:

15-1/2 oz. can black beans, drained
1 c. jicama, chopped
3/4 c. crumbled feta cheese
3 T. lime juice

1/3 c. fresh cilantro, chopped
2 t. green onions, minced
2 t. honey
1/4 c. red pepper flakes

Mix all ingredients well.

Swift autumn, like a bonfire of leaves.

-Elinor Wylie

October Bisque

Mary Murray
Gooseberry Patch

A velvety smooth soup, so pretty served in a vintage soup tureen.

1 onion, chopped
1/4 c. butter
4 c. chicken broth
28-oz. can whole tomatoes

1 T. sugar
2 15-oz. cans pumpkin
2 T. fresh parsley, chopped
2 T. fresh chives, chopped

Sauté onion in butter until onion is tender. Add broth and simmer for 15 minutes. Place tomatoes in a blender or food processor and blend until smooth. Add tomato mixture, sugar, pumpkin, parsley and chives to broth; heat through. Makes 8 servings.

A pickup truck tailgate makes a fine potluck buffet table. Fill the back with a galvanized tub of ice and soda, baskets of plates, napkins and silverware and lots of food…dinner country style!

Broccoli Cornbread

Carlotta McTigue
East Prairie, MO

Cut into large squares and top with a dollop of sour cream or salsa if you'd like.

1 c. butter, melted
12-oz. container cottage cheese
4 eggs, beaten
2 c. plus 1/3 c. cornmeal, divided
1/4 c. sugar

1 onion, chopped
10-oz. pkg. frozen chopped broccoli
1 c. shredded Cheddar cheese
1/4 c. oil

Combine butter, cottage cheese and eggs; blend in 2 cups cornmeal, sugar, onion, broccoli and Cheddar cheese. Pour oil into a large, oven-proof saucepan or cast iron skillet; tilt pan to evenly distribute oil. Sprinkle in remaining cornmeal. Over medium-high heat, pour in cornbread mixture. Bake at 375 degrees for 45 minutes or until golden. Serves 6 to 8.

For trouble-free covered dishes, pack food in a simple serving dish that can go from oven or refrigerator straight to the table...keep it simple!

Glazed Carrots

Stephanie Mayer
Portsmouth, VA

Carrots in a butter sauce. Eating your veggies has never been so easy!

1-1/2 lbs. carrots, peeled and
   sliced
1 T. unsalted butter
1/2 t. salt

1/2 c. water
2 T. cider
1 T. cider vinegar

Combine carrots, butter, salt and water in a saucepan. Bring to a boil, reduce heat and simmer, covered, for 10 minutes. Uncover; add cider and vinegar. Bring to a boil, stirring often to prevent sticking. Lower heat and simmer 15 minutes to reduce liquid to a glaze. Serves 4.

Hazelnut-Pumpkin Drop Biscuits

Shelly Turner
Boise, ID

Yummy, pumpkin biscuits...perfect alongside any soup.

1 c. hazelnuts, coarsely chopped
   and toasted
2 c. all-purpose flour
2 T. brown sugar, packed
2 t. baking powder
1/2 t. baking soda

1/4 t. salt
3 T. chilled butter, cut into pieces
3 T. shortening, chilled
1 c. canned pumpkin
1/4 c. milk

Combine first 6 ingredients; cut in butter and shortening until mixture resembles oatmeal. Stir in pumpkin and milk until a soft dough forms. Drop by rounded tablespoonfuls one inch apart onto a lightly greased baking sheet. Bake at 400 degrees for 15 minutes. Makes 2 dozen.

Spaghetti Squash Salad

Nancy Roschi
Lipon, WI

If you've never tried spaghetti squash, you really should!

2-1/2 lb. spaghetti squash, halved
1 onion, chopped
1 c. celery, diced
1/2 c. red pepper, chopped
1/2 c. green pepper, chopped
1/2 c. oil
1/4 c. vinegar
1 c. sugar
1/2 t. salt

Place squash cut side down in an ungreased 13"x9" baking pan; fill pan with 1/2-inch hot water. Bake at 350 degrees for 30 to 40 minutes; cool. Scoop out the center and and spoon into a serving bowl; discard seeds and shells. Mix in remaining ingredients; cover and chill for at least 2 hours. Serves 4.

Crisp fall days, antiquing and picnicking seem to go together. After a day of treasure-hunting with friends, break up the day to enjoy a packable feast. Keep it simple…sandwiches, thermoses of soup and cookies to nibble on will be plenty.

Party Potato Casserole

Sonja Bury
Rehoboth, MA

I rely on this casserole for all special get-togethers and holidays. Everyone just loves it and there are never any leftovers...guaranteed!

2 16-oz. bags frozen
   hashbrowns, thawed
3/4 c. margarine, melted and
   divided
1 t. salt
1/4 t. pepper

1/2 c. onion, chopped
10-3/4 oz. can cream of chicken
   soup
2 c. sour cream
2 c. Cheddar cheese, grated
2 c. corn flake cereal, crushed

In a large bowl, combine potatoes, 1/2 cup margarine, salt, pepper, onion, soup, sour cream and cheese. Place in a greased 13"x9" baking pan. Mix crushed cereal with remaining melted margarine and sprinkle over potato mixture. Bake, uncovered, at 350 degrees for one hour. Serves 12.

Pack goodies for a family gathering in an old bushel basket. Sturdy, easy to carry and roomy enough to hold all the potluck essentials like napkins, cups, plates and silverware.

Indian Summer Potluck

Squash & Apples

Autumn Dahlquist
Lake City, MI

This is a recipe we make at every fall family gathering. It always makes me think of home and family.

1 butternut squash, peeled and
    sliced
5 apples, cored, peeled and
    sliced

1/2 c. butter
1 c. brown sugar, packed
1 t. cinnamon

Arrange squash and apples in a greased 13"x9" baking pan; dot with butter. Sprinkle with brown sugar and cinnamon. Bake at 350 degrees for 45 minutes to one hour, or until tender. Serves 4 to 6.

Make your Indian Summer Potluck a progressive dinner. It's fun to move from house-to-house and visit with friends!

Cinnamon Crisps

Sharon Tillman
Hampton, VA

Dip these yummy crisps in apple butter or applesauce...a scrumptious treat!

1 T. hot water
1/2 t. vanilla extract
3 T. sugar

1/2 t. cinnamon
4 6-inch flour tortillas

Combine water and vanilla in a small bowl; set aside. Blend sugar and cinnamon together; set aside. Cut each tortilla into 6 triangles. Brush both sides with the vanilla mixture; sprinkle with the cinnamon-sugar mixture. Place tortillas on a baking sheet coated with non-stick vegetable spray. Bake at 450 degrees for 5 minutes or until crispy. Makes 2 dozen.

Set aside time for a little crafting after all the tasty food has been enjoyed. Choose a favorite theme, like card making, and everyone can bring along their favorite supplies to share.

Farm Apple Butter

Gina Marrone
Winston, GA

This oh-so-easy apple butter recipe can be refrigerated up to 2 months...but you'll eat it sooner than that!

3 lbs. Macintosh apples, cored, peeled and sliced
3 c. cider
1/4 c. honey

1/4 c. brown sugar, packed
1 t. cinnamon
1/2 t. allspice
1/8 t. ground cloves

Bring apples and cider to a boil in a large saucepan; reduce heat and simmer 20 minutes or until apples are soft. Stir in honey, brown sugar, cinnamon, allspice and cloves; mix well. Simmer for an additional 45 minutes to one hour, until apples break down into a very thick sauce. Cool just until warm; purée in batches in a blender. If consistency is too watery, return to saucepan and simmer until thickened. Cover and refrigerate. Makes about 2 pints.

Keep potluck menus casual and kid-friendly. Just for fun, use cookie cutters in fall shapes to cut out biscuits, bread or pats of butter.

Chocolate Pecan Pie

Debi DeVore
Dover, OH

A winning combination...ooey, gooey pecan pie and chocolate!

8 sqs. semi-sweet baking chocolate, divided
2 T. butter
9-inch pie crust
3 eggs, beaten and divided

1/4 c. brown sugar, packed
1 c. corn syrup
1 t. vanilla extract
1-1/2 c. pecan halves

Coarsely chop 4 squares of chocolate and set aside. In a large bowl, microwave remaining chocolate and butter together on high for one to 3 minutes or until butter is melted. Stir well until chocolate is completely melted. Brush bottom of pie crust with a small amount of beaten egg; set aside. Stir sugar, corn syrup, eggs and vanilla into chocolate mixture; blend. Add nuts and chopped chocolate. Pour into pie crust and bake at 350 degrees for 55 minutes or until knife inserted 2 inches from the edge of the crust comes out clean. Cool on wire rack. Serves 8.

It's easy to tote pies to a carry-in...top off the filled pie plate with a lightweight vintage pie pan and secure the two with jute.

Pumpkin Fudge

Linda Stone
Crookeville, TN

A really terrific fall treat.

5-oz. can evaporated milk
2-1/2 c. sugar
15-oz. can pumpkin, divided
1 t. cinnamon or pumpkin pie
   spice

7-oz. jar marshmallow creme
2 T. butter
6-oz. pkg. white chocolate chips
1 t. vanilla extract

Bring milk and sugar to a boil in a saucepan over medium heat. Stir with a wooden spoon. Mix in 3/4 of the can of pumpkin, reserving the rest for another recipe; stir in spice. Return to a boil; add marshmallow creme and butter and bring to a rolling boil. Boil, stirring often, for 18 minutes. Remove from heat. Add chocolate chips and vanilla; stir until creamy. Line a 9"x9" baking pan with plastic wrap; pour into prepared pan and let cool. Cut into squares. Makes about 6-1/2 dozen.

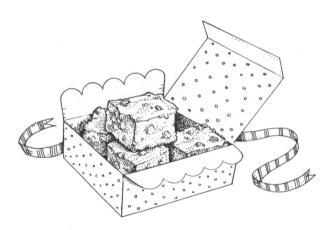

Tuck after-dinner candies inside hollowed-out walnut shells!
Tie shells closed with string and pile in a leaf-filled bowl and
guests can help themselves.

Sweet Potato Pie

Jacqueline Kurtz
Reading, PA

An old-time recipe that's tried & true.

15-oz. can sweet potatoes,
    drained and mashed
3 eggs, beaten
1 c. sugar
1 T. butter, melted

9-inch pie crust
Optional: 1/2 c. pecans,
    chopped; 1 c. mini
    marshmallows

Combine sweet potatoes, eggs, sugar and butter in a large bowl; stir until well blended. Pour into pie crust and bake at 350 degrees for one hour. If desired, remove from oven 5 minutes early and top with pecans and marshmallows; return to oven until marshmallows are golden. Serves 6.

Easy dress-ups for bake & take pies...before baking use a springerle pin to press out extra dough, cut around shapes and "glue" to pie edges with corn syrup. For icebox pies, make chocolate curls by pulling a vegetable peeler across a bar of chocolate, and top baked pies with sugared pecans or cranberries, so yummy!

Slow-Cooker Apple Pie

Samantha Starks
Madison, WI

Believe it...yummy apple pie prepared in a slow cooker!

8 tart apples, cored, peeled and
   sliced
1-1/4 t. cinnamon
1/4 t. allspice
1/4 t. nutmeg
3/4 c. milk
2 T. butter, softened
3/4 c. sugar

2 eggs
1 t. vanilla extract
1-1/2 c. biscuit baking mix,
   divided
1/3 c. brown sugar, packed
3 T. chilled butter

Toss apples with cinnamon, allspice and nutmeg. Place in a lightly greased slow cooker. Combine milk, softened butter, sugar, eggs, vanilla and 1/2 cup biscuit baking mix; spoon over apples. Combine remaining biscuit baking mix and brown sugar; cut in chilled butter until crumbly. Sprinkle over mixture in slow cooker; do not stir. Cover and cook on low setting 6 to 7 hours or until apples are tender. Serves 6 to 8.

Keep dessert time no-fuss. Brew a pot of steaming coffee or spiced cider, then pour into a thermal carafe. Easy to tote on a tray along with cream, sugar, mugs and spoons.

Schoolhouse Cookie Bars

Constance Paustian
New Ulm, MN

When I was an elementary school teacher, my principal's wife would make these for her family and for my classroom. To this day I think of her and my younger days as a teacher whenever I make them!

18-1/2 oz. pkg. yellow cake mix
2 c. quick-cooking oats,
   uncooked
3/4 c. oil
1 egg, beaten

12-oz. jar caramel ice cream
   topping
1 c. chocolate chips
Optional: 1/2 c. chopped nuts

Combine cake mix, oats, oil and egg; spread half of mixture into a greased 13"x9" baking pan. Drizzle with caramel topping; sprinkle with chocolate chips and nuts. Crumble remaining cake mix mixture over the top; bake at 350 degrees for 28 to 30 minutes. Cut into squares. Makes 18 to 20 servings.

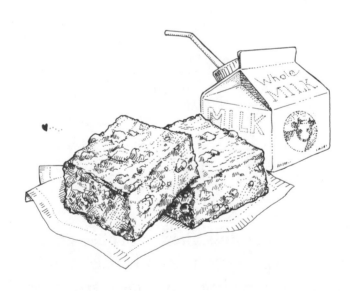

fall
FESTIVALS

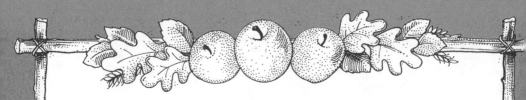

Savory Grilled Roastin' Ears

Nancy Wise
Little Rock, AR

There's nothing like the taste of grilled corn...give it a try!

12 ears corn in husks	1/2 c. butter, melted
2 qts. water	salt and pepper to taste

Soak ears of corn in water for several hours. Peel back the husk; remove the silk. Wrap husk back around ear and place on a hot grill, turning occasionally. Grill for one hour letting outer husk blacken; remove from grill using hot pads. Peel back husks. Brush with butter; add salt and pepper to taste. Makes 12 servings.

For added variety, serve herbal butters to drizzle over ears of roasted corn. Blend softened butter with freshly chopped herbs such as rosemary, chives, thyme or mint, adding as much or as little as desired.

Fall Festivals

Italian-Style Sausage Sandwiches

Robin Hill
Rochester, NY

Wrap 'em up in foil to serve...just like at the fair.

2 1-lb. pkgs. precooked Italian
   sausages
1/4 c. oil
2 green peppers, cut into strips
1 to 2 onions, sliced into rings

1/2 t. dried oregano
1/4 t. pepper
12 Italian-style rolls, split and
   toasted

In a large skillet over medium heat, sauté sausage in oil about
10 minutes, until heated through; remove from skillet and set aside.
Place peppers and onions in skillet; sprinkle with oregano and pepper
and sauté until tender, about 10 minutes. Serve sausages in toasted
rolls, topped with peppers and onions. Makes 12 servings.

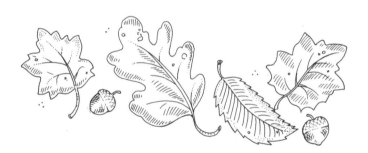

Take a walk on a crisp Autumn day to gather the prettiest
leaves. Preserved in glycerin, they'll make a beautiful
centerpiece all season long. Place leaves in a single layer in a
flat pan. Cover leaves with a mixture of one part glycerin and
two parts water. Use a rock to keep the leaves submerged for
one week, then remove and dry with paper towels.

Frosty Lemon Shake

Jo Ann

The kids just love this and they can easily make it at home.

1/2 c. sugar
2 lemons, juiced and 1/2 lemon
   reserved

crushed ice
water

Place sugar in a 16-ounce glass. Add lemon juice to glass, drop in one lemon half. Add ice to taste, fill with water. Cover and shake well. Serves one.

Harvest home, harvest home!

We've plowed, we've sowed

We've reaped, we've mowed

And brought safe home

Every load.

-Old Harvest Home Song

Soft Bread Sticks

Kris Warner
Circleville, OH

Our family loves these dipped in warm pizza sauce.

1 pkg. active dry yeast
1 c. warm water
3 T. sugar
1 t. salt

1/4 c. oil
3 c. all-purpose flour, divided
cornmeal

Dissolve yeast in water; add sugar, salt and oil, stirring until dissolved. Add 2 cups flour; beat until smooth. Stir in enough remaining flour to form a soft dough. Turn onto a floured surface; knead for 6 to 8 minutes or until smooth. Place in a greased bowl; cover. Let rise for one hour; punch dough down. Divide into 12 portions; roll each into a 10"x1/2" strip. Place on greased baking sheets lightly sprinkled with cornmeal; let rise for 45 minutes to one hour. Place baking sheets and a pan filled with boiling water in the oven. Bake at 400 degrees for 10 minutes or until golden. Makes one dozen.

Soft Bread Sticks, warm from the oven, are yummy! When making them, shake up the original recipe a little by sprinkling them, after baking, with cinnamon or powdered sugar, maple syrup or honey.

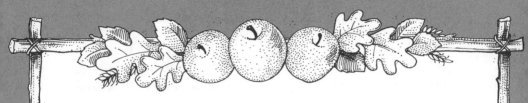

Hot Chicken Sandwiches

Kelly Alderson
Erie, PA

Spooned onto soft buns, this is a Midwestern favorite!

2-1/2 to 3-lb. chicken
6 T. butter
6 T. all-purpose flour
1 t. salt

1/8 t. pepper
1/2 c. celery, thinly sliced
12 sandwich buns, toasted

Place chicken in a Dutch oven, cover with water and bring to a boil. Reduce heat and simmer one hour, or until juices run clear when chicken is pierced. Reserve 2-1/2 cups chicken broth. Allow chicken to cool; remove skin and bones and shred meat. Melt butter in a saucepan; whisk in flour until smooth. Blend over low heat. Stir in reserved broth; boil one minute. Add salt and pepper; stir in celery and chicken. Heat thoroughly; serve on toasted buns. Makes 12 servings.

BIGGEST Pumpkin

On your next outing to a festival or fair, be sure to take in all the excitement with a scavenger hunt. For example: find the biggest vegetable, ride a carousel, smell the blooms at the flower show and taste something new. What fun you'll have chatting all the way home!

Firehouse Chicken

Noreen King
New Baltimore, MT

Serve over rice or noodles for a complete meal.

4 c. dry bread crumbs
1 lb. chicken cutlets, pounded
   thin
2 t. dried parsley
1/2 c. grated Parmesan cheese
1/2 lb. sliced mozzarella

10-3/4 oz. can cream of chicken
   soup
3 T. mayonnaise
3/4 c. water
3/4 c. shredded mozzarella

Coat the cutlets with bread crumbs; sprinkle with parsley and Parmesan cheese. Place a mozzarella slice in the center of each. Roll up cutlets, fasten with a toothpick, and arrange in a greased 13"x9" baking pan. In a separate bowl, mix soup, mayonnaise and water. Pour over cutlets and top with shredded mozzarella. Bake at 375 degrees for one hour. Makes 4 to 6 servings.

Why not pack a picnic tin with hearty food and sweet treats, then deliver to a local firehouse? What a welcome surprise!

Deep-Fried Veggies

Teresa Beal
Bowling Green, KY

The ideal batter for deep-fried zucchini, pickles, onion rings or mushrooms...all those "fair favorites!"

3/4 c. cornmeal
3/4 c. all-purpose flour
3 T. sugar
1 egg
non-alcoholic beer

oil for deep frying
variety of favorite vegetables,
  sliced as desired
salt to taste

Combine cornmeal, flour, sugar and egg. Add enough non-alcoholic beer to bring mixture to a medium consistency. Add oil to a deep fryer set at 350 degrees. Dip veggies into batter; fry until batter is golden and sprinkle with salt. Makes 4 to 6 servings.

Trivia buffs tell us, that in addition to Deep-Fried Veggies, there are more than 25 other deep-fried favorites at the average fair. The latest rage? Deep-fried candy bars!

Coney Island Hot Dog Sauce

Wendy Lee Paffenroth
Pine Island, NY

For a real fair favorite, top your coney with the works...coney sauce,
chopped onions, mustard and relish!

1 lb. ground beef, browned
2 t. chili powder
2 t. dried cumin
1 T. paprika
1 t. dried oregano

1/4 to 1/2 t. red pepper flakes
1/4 t. pepper
1 T. onion, diced
1/8 t. ground cloves
2 c. water

Mix all ingredients together in a skillet. Cover and simmer, stirring occasionally, until liquid has reduced to sauce consistency. Makes enough sauce for 6 to 12 hot dogs.

When hosting a family reunion, turn old-fashioned county fair activities into family fun! A spelling bee, cake walk, hoop rolling contest and even a raffle make for a great day of memory making.

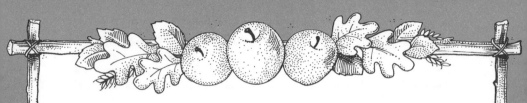

Paula's Tomato Pizza

Paula Spain
Warren, OH

No small slices of this pizza! Cut it into really big slices...just like the festival vendors like to sell them.

1 T. olive oil
12-inch thin pizza crust
garlic salt to taste
1 T. Italian seasoning
4 oz. shredded mozzarella
    cheese, divided
4 oz. crumbled feta cheese,
    divided

3 to 4 plum or roma tomatoes,
    sliced
1/8 c. grated Parmesan cheese
2 green peppers, sliced
2 hot peppers, sliced
4-oz. can sliced black olives

Spread olive oil over pizza crust. Sprinkle with garlic salt and Italian seasoning, then with half the mozzarella and feta cheese. Arrange tomatoes on crust without overlapping. Sprinkle with remaining mozzarella and feta cheese. Sprinkle with Parmesan; layer with peppers and olives. Bake 15 to 17 minutes at 375 degrees. Makes 8 servings.

Let the kids make mini pizzas that are just their size. Instead of dough, use bagels and English muffins...easy for little hands to hold on to.

Corn Dogs

Kay Marone
Des Moines, IA

For kids, the highlight of summer is going to the fair where enjoying corn dogs can be as exciting as riding the rides!

1 c. flour
2 T. sugar
1-1/2 t. baking powder
1 t. salt
2/3 c. cornmeal
2 T. shortening

1 egg
3/4 c. milk
8 to 10 hot dogs
8 to 10 wooden sticks
oil for deep frying

Combine flour, sugar, baking powder and salt; stir in cornmeal. Using a pastry cutter or 2 forks, cut in shortening until coarse crumbs form; set aside. Blend together egg and milk in a separate bowl. Stir into cornmeal mixture. Thoroughly dry each hot dog with a paper towel to ensure batter will cling. Insert a stick into each; dip in batter. Deep-fry in 350 to 375-degree oil for 4 to 5 minutes or until golden. Makes 8 to 10 servings.

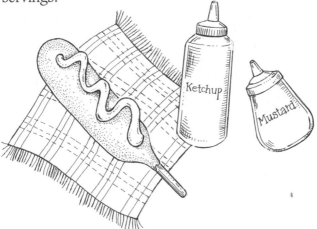

Give Corn Dogs a new spin by using Italian sausage or bratwurst instead of hot dogs.

Garlic Oven Fries

Janet Pastrick
Fairfax, VA

Serve these up in tall paper cups...another favorite way to bring the feel of county fairs right to your kitchen!

4 baking potatoes
4 T. extra-virgin olive oil
2 t. salt

1 t. freshly ground pepper
1-1/2 T. garlic

Scrub and rinse potatoes well; cut lengthwise into 1/2-inch wide slices. Place in a medium bowl and toss with olive oil, salt, pepper and garlic. Arrange potato slices on an ungreased baking sheet in a single layer. Bake at 400 degrees until potatoes are golden on the bottom, about 30 minutes. Turn over and continue baking until golden all over, another 15 minutes. Serve immediately. Makes 4 servings.

Top Garlic Oven Fries with melted cheese to make the easiest cheesy fries, or top them with salt and vinegar...another festival must-have!

Fried Green Tomatoes

Zona Hill
New Albany, IN

These are sooo good! We have a garden every year and as soon as the tomatoes are the right size, we have to make this recipe.

1-1/2 c. all-purpose flour, divided
1-1/2 c. buttermilk
2 eggs
1 t. salt, divided

1 t. pepper, divided
3 green tomatoes, sliced into 4 to 6 slices
2 c. oil

Whisk together one tablespoon flour, buttermilk, eggs, 1/2 teaspoon salt and 1/2 teaspoon pepper. In a second bowl, blend remaining flour, salt and pepper. Heat oil until very hot in a heavy skillet. Dip tomato slices into buttermilk mixture, dredge in flour mixture and heat in oil until golden on each side. Drain on paper towel; serve warm. Makes 4 to 6 servings.

Try using red tomatoes in our Fried Green Tomatoes recipe...with a slightly sweeter taste, they're sure to be another favorite.

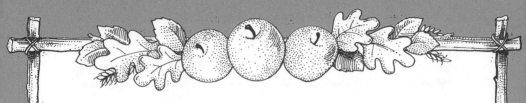

Blue-Ribbon Pickled Beets

Gail Prather
Bethel, MN

Not only a simple canning recipe, but a blue ribbon winner, too!

1 T. mixed pickling spice
2 c. sugar
2 6-inch cinnamon sticks
1-1/2 t. salt
2 c. red wine vinegar
1-1/2 c. white vinegar

1-1/2 c. water
3 qts. beets, peeled and cooked
3 1-qt. canning jars and lids,
   sterilized

Tie pickling spice in a cheesecloth bag; place in a large saucepan and add all ingredients except beets. Bring mixture to a boil; reduce heat and simmer 15 minutes. Remove and discard cinnamon sticks and spice bag. Pack beets into jars, leaving 1/4-inch headspace. Ladle liquid over beets, leaving 1/4-inch headspace. Remove any air bubbles. Wipe rims; secure lids and rings. Process 30 minutes in a boiling water bath. Set aside to cool; check for seals. Makes 3 quarts.

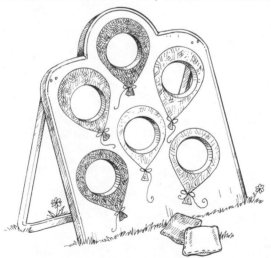

Invite friends and neighbors over for a backyard festival.
Games like a hay bale toss, sack races, Red Rover
and 3-legged races add old-fashioned fun!

Zucchini Relish

Michelle Campen
Peoria, IL

Great combinations...serve Zucchini Relish with cheese-filled potato skins, use as a dip for bagel chips or serve over a block of cream cheese as an all-time favorite appetizer.

6 to 8 zucchini, peeled and
    cubed
4 onions, chopped
4 green peppers, chopped
4 red peppers, chopped
5 T. salt
1 t. turmeric
2 T. cornstarch

1/2 t. alum
2 t. celery seed
1 t. nutmeg
1 t. dry mustard
2-1/2 c. vinegar
6 c. sugar
7 1-pt. canning jars and lids,
    sterilized

Grind zucchini in food grinder or food processor; measure 10 cups into a large stockpot. Grind onions and peppers; combine with zucchini. Sprinkle with salt; pour zucchini mixture into a large mixing bowl; let stand overnight. Rinse and drain well; set aside. Stir together remaining ingredients in stockpot; bring to a boil. Add zucchini mixture; simmer gently for 30 minutes. Pack in jars, leaving 1/4-inch headspace, and seal. Wipe rims; secure lids and rings. Process 30 minutes in a boiling water bath. Set aside to cool; check for seals. Makes 7 pints.

One-pint jars of Zucchini Relish are just the right size for gift giving...share jars with friends during the holidays to give them a taste of summer.

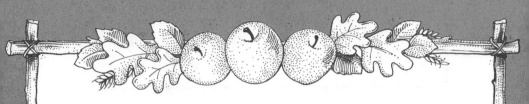

Country-Style Vanilla Ice Cream

Kristina Wyatt
Madera, CA

Bring the county fair to your kids any time of year...set up an ice cream stand right in the kitchen. Bring out the sprinkles, jimmies, hot fudge and caramel sauces, maraschino cherries and nuts. Yummy!

4 eggs
2-1/2 c. sugar
2 T. vanilla extract

1/4 t. salt
4 c. whipping cream
5 c. milk

Beat eggs in a mixing bowl until foamy; gradually blend in sugar, vanilla and salt. Mix until thickened; set aside. Combine cream and milk in a saucepan; heat until steam rises from the pan. Blend in egg mixture; cook for 5 more minutes. Bring to room temperature; refrigerate for at least one hour. Pour into an electric ice cream maker; freeze according to manufacturer's instructions. Makes 4 quarts.

Don't miss the butter sculptures at the fair; kids love 'em!
Usually found in the dairy building, this tradition began in
1903 when the first butter cow was made
using 880 pounds of butter.

Peach Cobbler

Becky Hall
Carthage, MO

No need to top with ice cream, but it does make it extra-special.

3-1/2 c. peaches, peeled and
    sliced
1 T. lemon juice
1 c. sugar

1/2 t. salt
1 c. all-purpose flour
1 egg, beaten
6 T. butter, melted

Place peaches in a lightly greased 10"x6" baking pan; sprinkle with lemon juice. Stir; set aside. Sift sugar, salt and flour together; add egg. Toss with a fork until mixture is crumbly; spread over peaches. Drizzle with butter; bake at 375 degrees for 35 to 40 minutes. Serves 6.

Stack bales of hay or rows of cornstalks in the backyard to create a maze…little ones will have a ball racing to find their way through!

Pumpkin Waffles

Lisa Kesselring
South Bloomingville, OH

We live in an 1860's log cabin in the middle of the woods. When the night air turns cool and the leaves change to their brilliant colors, I know what my family will be requesting for breakfast, Pumpkin Waffles! They're wonderful and make the whole cabin smell like Fall.

2 c. all-purpose flour	4 eggs, separated
2 T. baking powder	1-1/2 c. milk
1 T. cinnamon	1 c. canned pumpkin
1/2 t. coriander	3/4 c. butter, melted
1/2 t. nutmeg	1 T. vanilla extract
1/4 t. salt	Garnish: butter, maple syrup

Combine flour, baking powder, spices and salt in a large mixing bowl; set aside. In a second bowl, beat egg yolks slightly; blend in milk, pumpkin, butter and vanilla. Add pumpkin mixture to flour mixture, stirring until just combined. In a small bowl, beat egg whites until stiff peaks form; gently fold into pumpkin mixture. Pour one to 1-1/2 cups batter onto a preheated, lightly greased waffle iron. Bake according to manufacturer's instructions. Repeat with remaining batter. Makes six, 9-inch waffles.

When served alongside waffles, pancakes or French toast, a pat of butter that's been pressed with a cookie stamp is sure to guarantee smiles!

Cinnamon Baked Pumpkin

Kathy Grashoff
Fort Wayne, IN

You just have to try this…it's fantastic!

3 T. brown sugar, packed
1 t. cinnamon
1/8 t. salt

1-1/2 lb. pie pumpkin, peeled
   and seeded
1 T. peanut oil

Stir together brown sugar, cinnamon and salt; set aside. Cut pumpkin into 1/4-inch by 2-1/2 inch slices; toss with oil. Arrange in a single layer in a greased 2-quart baking dish. Sprinkle sugar mixture evenly over slices, cover and bake at 350 degrees for 30 minutes. Uncover and stir pumpkin slices. Bake, uncovered, for 15 to 20 additional minutes or until tender. Makes 6 to 8 servings.

Fun fall festival trivia…did you know a
prize-winning pumpkin gains about 40 pounds
a day at its peak growing time?

Microwave Caramel Corn

Sally Borland
Port Gibson, NY

A kid-pleasing recipe ready in almost no time!

8 c. popped popcorn
1/2 c. brown sugar, packed
1/2 c. butter
2 T. corn syrup

1/4 t. salt
1/4 t. baking soda
1/4 t. vanilla extract

Divide popped corn into two 2-quart microwaveable bowls; set aside. Combine brown sugar, butter, corn syrup and salt in a one-quart microwaveable bowl. Microwave on high for 1-1/2 minutes. Stir and microwave an additional 2 minutes, stirring after one minute. Add baking soda and vanilla; stir well. Divide cooked syrup and pour half over each bowl of popped corn, mixing well. Microwave each bowl for 2 minutes, stirring after one minute. Watch to make sure it doesn't burn. Cool and break into pieces. Makes 8 servings.

A leaf rubbing makes such a pretty bookmark; what a sweet gift for a friend. Place a leaf between 2 sheets of paper. Remove the wrapper from a crayon, turn the crayon on its side and gently rub over the top sheet of paper. Use decorative-edged scissors to trim.

Caramel-Marshmallow Apples

Jessica Parker
Mulvane, KS

Candy apples are so simple to make, you can treat yourself any time.

14-oz. pkg. caramels, unwrapped	1 T. water
1 c. mini marshmallows	5 to 6 wooden sticks
	5 to 6 apples

Combine caramels, marshmallows and water in a saucepan; heat until caramels melt. Cool slightly. Insert sticks into apples; dip in caramel mixture until well coated. Place on a baking sheet lined with buttered wax paper; refrigerate until firm. Makes 5 to 6.

Apples are terrific with almost any topping! Try drizzling with melted chocolate and rolling in crushed cookies or dipping in white chocolate and rolling in pecans or slivered almonds…yummy!

Peach Smoothies

April King
Eugene, OR

Try strawberries instead of peaches and sprinkle in a little cinnamon!

2 c. milk
2 c. frozen sliced peaches
1/4 c. frozen orange juice
   concentrate

1 T. sugar
5 to 6 ice cubes
1/4 t. vanilla extract

Combine all ingredients in a blender container; cover and blend until smooth. Serves 4.

Festivals always seem to have a flea market where treasures are just waiting to be taken home. Be sure to tote along a backpack to tuck "must-haves" into and to keep hands free for shopping.

Autumn
SOUP SUPPER

Maple Autumn Squash Soup

Vickie

The best flavors of Fall in one soup. You might want to make it a couple of days ahead and refrigerate so the flavors can blend, then slowly reheat.

1 lb. butternut squash, peeled, cubed and boiled
1/2 c. butter, divided
1/4 c. maple syrup
3 T. brown sugar, packed
1 t. cinnamon
1/2 t. ground ginger
3 T. all-purpose flour
2 c. chicken broth
2 c. unsweetened applesauce
1 c. Granny Smith apples, cored, peeled and chopped
2 c. light cream
salt and pepper to taste

Combine squash with 4 tablespoons butter, syrup, brown sugar and spices; mash well and set aside. Melt remaining butter in a large pot over medium heat; add flour and cook for 3 minutes, stirring constantly. Blend in broth and cook until soup thickens. Stir in squash mixture, applesauce and apples. Cook over medium heat until warmed through, stirring often. Add cream and heat just until soup begins to bubble around the edges. Cool and refrigerate overnight. Reheat over medium heat until warmed through. Makes 6 to 8 servings.

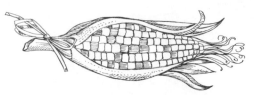

Soup Suppers are a fuss-free way to get together with friends, neighbors and family. Set up a buffet table, decorate simply with gourds, pumpkins, cornstalks and mums and it's all set. Each family brings a favorite soup to share, along with the recipe. What a delicious way to try a variety of soups and maybe find a new favorite!

Harvest Corn Chowder

Pat Habiger
Spearville, KS

In our family, this is always a winner on a chilly day.

1 onion, chopped
1 red pepper, chopped
1-1/2 t. minced garlic
1/2 t. poultry seasoning
1/4 t. dried thyme, crushed
1 T. olive oil
4-oz. pkg. ham, chopped
2 potatoes, peeled and cut into
    1/2-inch cubes

2 c. water
1 T. chicken bouillon granules
1-1/2 c. frozen corn, thawed
1 c. chicken, cooked and cubed
1-1/2 c. milk
3/4 c. half-and-half

In a saucepan, sauté onion, pepper, garlic, poultry seasoning and thyme in oil for 5 minutes; add ham. Heat for an additional 5 minutes; stir in potatoes, water and bouillon. Bring to a boil; reduce heat and simmer for 10 minutes. Mix in corn, chicken, milk and half-and-half; heat until warmed through. Serves 5.

Just for fun, use a hollowed-out pumpkin as a soup tureen, but try something unexpected. An all-white Lumina pumpkin or a plump green & orange Cinderella pumpkin make the prettiest presentations!

Sweet Potato Biscuits

Paula Hicks
Camden, AR

A great way to use up leftover mashed sweet potatoes!

2 c. all-purpose flour
2/3 c. sugar
2 T. baking powder
1-1/2 t. salt

1/2 c. shortening
2 c. sweet potatoes, cooked,
   peeled, mashed
1/4 c. buttermilk

Sift flour, sugar, baking powder and salt together; cut in shortening.
Mix in potatoes and milk; turn out onto a lightly floured board. Knead
lightly; roll out 1/2-inch thick. Cut with a biscuit cutter; arrange on
greased baking sheets. Bake at 475 degrees for 12 to 15 minutes.
Makes 2 dozen.

Soup for Supper

Making invitations to a Soup Supper doesn't need to take a
lot of time to make them extra special. Tie a mailing tag with
all the get-together details around the handle of a spoon or
stem of a gourd and deliver...done in no time!

Wisconsin Cheese Soup

Kelly Simpson
Rapid City, SD

Remember not to use low-fat cheese, it just won't have the same rich, creamy and flavorful taste.

5 T. butter
2 stalks celery, chopped
1/2 green pepper, chopped
5 mushrooms, chopped
2 carrots, chopped
1 onion, chopped
1/2 c. ham, chopped
1/2 c. all-purpose flour
2 T. cornstarch

1 qt. chicken broth
1 qt. milk
1/2 t. paprika
1/2 t. mustard
16-oz. pkg. shredded sharp
    Cheddar cheese
1/4 to 1/2 t. cayenne pepper
salt and pepper to taste

Melt butter in a stockpot; add celery, green pepper, mushrooms, carrot, onion and ham. Cook for 10 minutes or until vegetables are tender; stir in flour and cornstarch. Heat for 3 minutes; pour in broth and stir until thickened. Mix in milk, mustard, cheese, cayenne pepper, salt and pepper; heat until cheese is melted. Makes 2-1/2 quarts.

Whip up a table centerpiece in seconds. Fill a shallow bowl with cool water and rows of garnet-red dahlias and little orange gourds...so colorful!

Carrot Soup

Gloria Warren
Ontario, Canada

This very hearty soup is always served with fresh crusty bread and is always so much in demand in our Canadian household I have to make a double batch!

6 carrots, peeled and sliced
2 potatoes, peeled and cubed
1-1/2 c. boiling water
2 cubes chicken bouillon
1 t. Worcestershire sauce
2 t. salt
1/4 t. pepper

1/2 t. paprika
1/2 onion, chopped
1/4 c. butter
3 T. all-purpose flour
3 c. milk
1/4 t. dried thyme
1/4 c. fresh parsley, chopped

Place carrots, potatoes and water in a large stockpot; add bouillon, Worcestershire sauce, salt, pepper and paprika. Bring to a boil; reduce heat and simmer for 15 minutes or until vegetables are tender; set aside. Sauté onion in butter; blend in flour. Pour in milk; bring to a boil. Stir into vegetable mixture; add thyme. Bring to a boil; reduce heat and simmer for 5 minutes. Add parsley. Serves 4.

After supper, celebrate the season with easy-to-make crafts. Set a worktable outside and carve pumpkins, make wreaths and garlands or fragrant potpourri...a great way to spend time together!

Autumn Soup Supper

Homemade Dinner Rolls

Romola Knotts
Woodstock, OH

A family favorite! I've always made a big batch for our family gatherings.

2 c. milk
1/8 t. salt
2 T. sugar
2 T. butter

2 pkgs. active dry yeast
1/2 c. warm water
5 to 6 c. flour
1/8 c. butter, melted

Bring milk and salt to a boil in a saucepan; stir in sugar and butter. Remove from heat; cool and set aside. Dissolve yeast in water; stir into milk mixture. Begin by adding 3 cups flour; gradually add remaining flour until stiff; knead. Let rise until double in bulk; roll into balls. Place on 2 greased 13"x9" baking pans; let rise again. Bake at 400 degrees for 12 to 15 minutes or until golden; brush with melted butter. Makes 2-1/2 to 3 dozen.

A Soup Supper menu shouldn't be fussy and the serving style is "help yourself!" A variety of soups, along with some biscuits and rolls and a crock of creamery butter is all that's needed. No kitchen duty at this gathering...the idea is to relax and enjoy the season together.

Cheesy Bacon-Wild Rice Soup

Terri Peterson
New Richmond, WI

The melted cheese makes this soup really delicious.

9 to 10 slices bacon, diced
1 onion, chopped
2 10-3/4 oz. cans cream of
    potato soup

1-1/2 c. prepared wild rice
2 pts. half-and-half
2 c. American cheese, shredded

Sauté bacon and onion together until bacon is crisp and onion is tender; drain and set aside. Combine soup and rice in a saucepan; stir in bacon mixture, half-and-half and cheese. Heat until cheese melts. Serves 6 to 8.

For this,
we are blessed
~·~o~·~
The love of company,
The company of friends
and all the abundance
of Autumn.

Old Blessing

Chicken Minestrone

Tara Pieron
Farmington, MI

This recipe takes a little time, but is well worth the result!

5 10-1/2 oz. cans chicken broth
1 T. tomato paste
1-1/2 t. hot pepper sauce
1 t. dried oregano
1/2 t. dried rosemary
1-1/2 c. butternut squash,
   peeled and diced
1 T. butter
1 T. oil

1 onion, diced
3 tomatoes, chopped
1/2 lb. spinach, chopped
15-oz. can chickpeas
1 c. fresh basil, sliced
2 cloves garlic, minced
2 c. chicken, cooked and diced
6-oz. pkg. cooked bowtie pasta

Bring broth to a boil in a large stockpot; add tomato paste, pepper sauce, oregano and rosemary. Stir in squash and cook for 10 minutes; set aside. Heat butter and oil in a skillet; add onions and sauté for 4 minutes. Stir in tomatoes and heat for 3 minutes; spoon into broth mixture. Stir in spinach and chickpeas; heat for about 10 minutes. Stir in basil, garlic, chicken and pasta; heat through. Serves 6.

If your Soup Supper is outdoors, toss a few colorful quilts and throws over the chairs...so cozy for snuggling under as the sun sets.

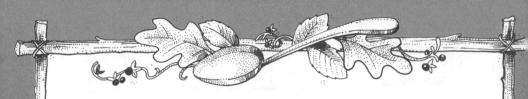

2-Bean Chowder

Gloria Robertson
Midland, TX

There's nothing like the aroma of simmering soup to warm up a crisp autumn day.

1 c. dry Great Northern beans
1 c. dry red beans
2 qts. water
8 slices bacon, crisply cooked
    and crumbled
1 c. onion, chopped

1 clove garlic, minced
3/4 c. celery, diced
3/4 c. carrot, diced
1/8 t. red pepper flakes
1-1/2 c. milk
salt and pepper to taste

Bring beans and water to a boil and boil for 2 minutes. Cover and let stand for one hour. Add bacon; cover and simmer for 1-1/2 hours. Remove from heat and mash a portion of the beans. Return to heat; stir in mashed beans, onion, garlic, celery, carrot and red pepper flakes. Cover and simmer for one hour. Add milk and heat through; season to taste with salt and pepper. Makes 6 to 8 servings.

Try serving soups and chowders in bread bowls...yummy! Scoop out small rye or sourdough bread rounds and brush the insides with olive oil. Bake in a 350-degree oven for 10 minutes, then fill with soup.

Autumn Soup Supper

Old-Fashioned Split Pea Soup

Judy Steinbach
Rancho Cordova, CA

Serve this up in large mugs with handles…makes it easy for the little ones to hold onto.

2-1/4 c. split peas
2-1/2 qts. water
2 ham bones
1-1/2 c. onion, chopped
1/4 t. garlic salt

1/4 t. dried marjoram
salt and pepper to taste
1 c. celery, chopped
1 c. carrots, chopped
1 t. dried parsley

Soak peas in water overnight; drain. Mix together peas, water, ham bones, onion, garlic salt, marjoram, salt and pepper in a stockpot. Bring to a boil; reduce heat and simmer for 2 hours. Remove ham bones; stir in celery, carrots and parsley. Simmer for 45 minutes or until vegetables are tender. Serves 8 to 10.

Here's how to make patterned pumpkin centerpieces in no time. Paint white rings of latex paint around a pale orange pumpkin to resemble a yellowware bowl, or stencil a favorite pattern on a white Lumina pumpkin. March them right down the center of the buffet table!

Barley Quick Bread

Sherry Saarinen
Hancock, MI

My two sisters and I traveled to Finland to visit the towns where our ancestors had lived. It was in Rovaniemi, at the Arctic Circle, where we first sampled this freshly baked bread...what a pleasant memory.

2 c. all-purpose flour
1/2 c. barley flour
1 t. salt
1 t. sugar

1 t. baking powder
1/2 t. baking soda
1 c. buttermilk
2 T. butter, melted

Combine flours, salt, sugar, baking powder and baking soda; add buttermilk. Knead on a floured surface; roll out to a 1/2 to 3/4-inch thick oval. Score with a knife; prick with a fork. Place on a greased and floured baking sheet; bake at 375 degrees for 15 to 25 minutes. Cool; brush with butter. Makes one loaf.

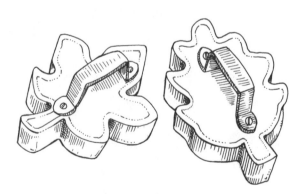

Cut slices of bread or biscuit dough with big maple or oak leaf-shaped cookie cutters...kid-friendly and festive!

Corn & Potato Chowder

Phyl Broich-Wessling
Garner, IA

Mmm, bacon, potatoes and carrots...a can't-fail recipe.

1 T. butter
3 to 4 slices bacon
1 c. onion, chopped
3/4 c. green pepper, chopped
1 T. garlic, minced
2 T. all-purpose flour
4 to 5 c. chicken broth
5 c. redskin potatoes, peeled and
    finely chopped

2 c. carrots, chopped
2 c. corn
1 c. heavy cream
1 t. fresh thyme or dill, chopped
2 T. fresh parsley, chopped
1/8 t. salt
1/8 t. pepper

Melt butter in a stockpot; add bacon and cook until crisp. Remove bacon and set aside; reserve 1/4 cup drippings and return to stockpot. Add onions and peppers and heat until tender; stir in garlic and heat one minute longer. Remove from heat and sprinkle in flour; blend well. Gradually stir in 4 cups broth; add more as needed to reach desired consistency. Stir in potatoes and carrots. Return stockpot to heat and simmer, covered, until vegetables are tender. Add corn, salt and pepper; cover and simmer 10 minutes longer. Stir in cream, herbs and reserved bacon; simmer 2 minutes. Makes 6 to 8 servings.

Of soup and love, the first is best.

-Spanish Proverb

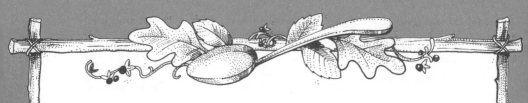

Old-Fashioned Tomato Soup

Fawn McKenzie
Wenatchee, WA

Go ahead, you know you want to serve this steaming soup alongside grilled cheese sandwiches...a terrific twosome!

32-oz. can diced tomatoes
1 c. chicken broth
2 T. butter
2 T. sugar

1 T. onion, chopped
1/8 t. baking soda
2 c. light cream

Combine tomatoes, broth, butter, sugar, onions and baking soda in a large stockpot. Simmer for one hour. Heat cream in a double boiler; add to hot tomato mixture. Blend well. Serves 4 to 6.

Oh-so clever! Alongside each slow cooker or soup tureen, use Scrabble® game pieces to spell out soup names. Guests will know just what's inside and it's a fun twist on the traditional table tent.

Maple-Glazed Muffins

Carol Hickman
Kingsport, TN

Tuck in a basket and deliver to your neighbor; what a sweet surprise.

2 eggs, beaten
1-2/3 c. sour cream
1-2/3 c. maple syrup, divided
1 c. all-purpose flour
1 c. bran flake cereal

1 t. baking soda
3/4 c. chopped pecans
6 T. butter, melted

Combine eggs, sour cream and one cup maple syrup; stir in bran flakes, baking soda and nuts. Fill paper-lined muffin cups 3/4 full. Bake at 400 degrees for 15 to 20 minutes. Combine remaining maple syrup and butter; dip muffins in mixture. Makes one dozen.

Soups can be garnished with lots of tasty toppers...toasted nuts, crispy crumbled bacon, sour cream, croutons, fresh herbs or shredded cheese. Try something new!

Honey-Wheat Bread

Pamela Peterson
Lake Isabella, CA

Serve warm spread with honey butter.

1 T. yeast
1/2 c. honey, divided
2-1/2 c. warm water, divided

1/3 c. olive oil
6 c. whole-wheat flour, divided
1 t. salt

Combine yeast, 1/4 cup honey and 1/2 cup water; set aside. Mix remaining water, remaining honey, oil, 3 cups flour and salt; add yeast mixture. Stir in remaining flour. Knead dough on a lightly floured surface for 10 minutes. Place dough in a large greased bowl; cover with a towel and let rise for 1-1/2 hours or until double in bulk; punch down. Separate dough into 2 equal portions; shape into loaves. Place in 2 greased 9"x5" loaf pans; cover and let rise 45 additional minutes. Bake at 350 degrees for 30 minutes. Remove to cool on wire racks; let cool 20 minutes before slicing. Makes 2 loaves.

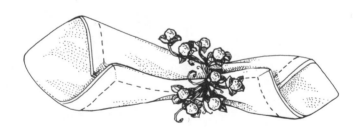

For a simple napkin ring, wrap napkins and silverware with bittersweet vines. If the bittersweet won't bend easily, run warm water over it and place in a paper bag to soften.

Mom's Creamy Chicken Chowder

Stephanie Swensen
Mapleton, UT

Paired with homemade bread or rolls, this is my family's most-requested soup.

12 c. chicken broth
3 cubes chicken bouillon
1 c. celery, diced
1/2 c. onion, diced
1-1/2 c. carrots, peeled and grated
1/2 c. butter
12-oz. can evaporated milk

1/2 c. water
1-1/2 c. all-purpose flour
4 to 6 boneless, skinless chicken breasts, cooked and cubed
3 c. potatoes, peeled, cubed and cooked

Combine broth, bouillon, celery, onion and carrots in a large pot; simmer until vegetables are tender. Stir in butter until melted; set aside. In a blender, mix milk, water and flour until smooth; add to soup mixture. Stir in chicken and potatoes and heat until warmed through. Serves 12 to 15.

Pour soup samples into a variety of thermoses and let guests help themselves. The soup will stay nice and warm and the thermoses can be tucked into a picnic basket for easy toting to and from supper.

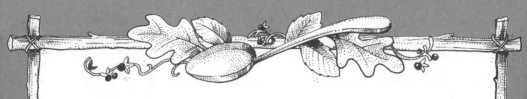

Stuffed Pepper Soup

Mary Lou Wincek
South Bend, IN

Try it! A new spin on a favorite combination of flavors.

2 lbs. ground beef, browned
8 c. water
28-oz. can diced tomatoes
28-oz. can tomato sauce
2 c. prepared long grain rice

2 c. green peppers, chopped
2 cubes beef bouillon
1/4 c. brown sugar, packed
2 t. salt
1 t. pepper

Mix together all ingredients in a stockpot; bring to a boil. Reduce heat and simmer for 30 to 40 minutes or until green peppers are tender. Serves 8 to 10.

Not enough soup bowls on hand for family & friends? Open the cupboards and pull out sturdy mugs! They're just as nice and the handles makes them easy to hold on to.

New England Clam Chowder

Joyce Galonski
Exeter, RI

A recipe shared with me by my mother-in-law. I created my own version by adding a few more ingredients and more butter.

2 c. onions, chopped
2 c. celery, chopped
1 c. butter
1-1/4 c. all-purpose flour
1 qt. minced clams
46-oz. can clam juice

8 potatoes, peeled, cubed and cooked
1 qt. half-and-half
2 T. dried parsley
salt and pepper to taste

Sauté onions and celery in butter in a saucepan until tender. Add flour; mix well, heat for 2 minutes and set aside. In a stockpot, combine clams and clam juice; bring to a boil, reduce heat and simmer for 20 minutes. Spoon some of the juice into onion mixture; stir until well blended. Stir into clam mixture; bring to a boil. Add potatoes, half-and-half and parsley; salt and pepper to taste. Heat through; do not boil. Serves 10 to 12.

Soups freeze well, so go ahead and make a recipe that serves a lot, then freeze in single-serving containers to enjoy later. What a time saver on a busy Saturday.

Andrea's Biscuits

Andrea Pocreva
San Antonio, TX

With only 3 ingredients, this is a time saving recipe you can count on.

1/2 c. butter, melted   2 c. biscuit baking mix
1 c. sour cream

Mix all ingredients together; pour into greased muffin cups. Bake at 350 degrees for 20 minutes. Makes 10.

Whimsical bottle-cap bowls were popular in the 1950's, so whip up a couple to hold rolls, muffins or biscuits. Using fine-grit sandpaper, remove the shiny finish from a wooden bowl. Coat the bowl with acrylic paint, let dry and spray on an acrylic sealer. Use hot glue to add rows of bottle caps around the bowl. Press the caps on for a few seconds to secure; it'll bowl 'em over!

Sour Cream-Potato Soup

Carole Wagner
Seven Valleys, PA

We like to serve this soup with a green salad and loaf of sourdough bread...always a hearty and filling dinner.

1 onion, chopped
1 T. butter
3 potatoes, cubed
4 c. water
1 T. parsley

1/2 c. all-purpose flour
1 c. sour cream
2 eggs
Garnish: hardboiled egg,
  chopped

Sauté onion in butter until tender; add potatoes, water and parsley. Heat until potatoes are tender; remove from heat. In a bowl, combine flour, sour cream and eggs; slowly stir into soup mixture. Heat through until eggs are set, stirring constantly. Garnish with chopped egg. Makes 6 servings.

Keep it simple...fill old-fashioned apple baskets with ice and bottles of frosty soda, cider or milk so everyone can choose their favorite. For warm spiced cider or coffee, use roomy insulated coffee or tea pots...no running to and from the kitchen to make more!

Great Boston Brown Bread

Barbara Tuve
Montvale, NJ

A dense bread that's yummy topped with apple butter or jam.

3 c. whole-wheat flour
2 t. baking soda
1 T. salt
2 c. brown sugar, packed

2 eggs, separated
2 c. buttermilk
1/2 c. raisins

Combine flour, baking soda and salt; add brown sugar, egg yolks and buttermilk. Stir in raisins; fold in egg whites. Fill greased and floured 16-ounce cans half full; bake at 350 degrees for 45 minutes. Let cool. Remove end of cans, push bread out and slice. Makes 2 to 3 loaves.

Set out jars of of jams & jellies to spread over slices of warm
bread…a sweet ending to any
Soup Supper get-together!

Baked Beef Stew

Patricia Dammrich
St. Louis, MO

*One thing I like about this recipe is I don't have to brown the meat.
It's so simple to prepare, makes its own gravy while it cooks and
the slice of bread is the secret ingredient.*

14-oz. can diced tomatoes
1 c. water
3 T. quick-cooking tapioca
2 t. sugar
1-1/2 t. salt
2 lbs. beef stew meat

4 carrots, chopped
3 potatoes, peeled and chopped
2 stalks celery, chopped
1 onion, chopped
1 slice bread, cubed

Combine tomatoes, water, tapioca, sugar, salt and pepper; add
remaining ingredients. Mix well; pour into a greased 13"x9" baking
pan. Cover; bake at 375 degrees for 2 hours. Serves 6 to 8.

Little sugar pumpkins are sweet soup bowls...the ideal size!

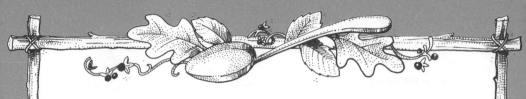

Julieanne's Chowder

Julieanne Young
Millinocket, ME

Haddock really adds an incredible flavor...you have to try this!

1/2 c. salt pork or bacon, diced
1 onion, diced
2 stalks celery, diced
4 potatoes, peeled and diced
8-oz. bottle clam juice

1-1/2 lb. haddock, rinsed
5-oz. can evaporated milk
pepper to taste
1-1/2 t. dried parsley
1 T. butter

Sauté salt pork or bacon in a Dutch oven until crisply cooked; remove and set aside. Add the onion and celery to the Dutch oven and sauté until translucent; remove and set aside. Place potatoes and clam juice in the Dutch oven. Cover with water; bring to a boil, reduce heat and simmer until soft. Add haddock; return to a boil, reduce heat and simmer for 5 minutes. Stir in milk, onion, celery, pepper and parsley. Heat through; stir in butter and heat until butter is melted. To serve, ladle potatoes and liquid into bowls. Add a piece of fish to each bowl; garnish with reserved salt pork or bacon. Serves 4.

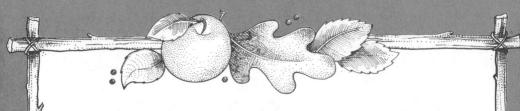

Celebration Pork Tenderloin

Jill Valentine
Jackson, TN

Start off an Oktoberfest celebration with this traditional favorite!

2 t. oil
1-lb. pork tenderloin, cut into
   1/4-inch slices
1 onion, sliced and separated
   into rings

1/4 c. vinegar
1 T. hot pepper sauce
1 T. brown sugar, packed
salt to taste

Heat oil in a 12-inch skillet on medium-high heat; lay pork slices in skillet and heat for about 5 minutes on one side. Arrange onion rings over pork. While the pork cooks, mix together the vinegar, pepper sauce and brown sugar. Microwave 30 seconds on high; stir to dissolve the sugar. Immediately pour mixture over the meat and onions. Turn pork slices over; continue to heat 5 more minutes or just until pork is cooked thoroughly. Season with salt to taste; serve at once topped with onion rings. Makes 4 servings.

Oompah-pah Sauerkraut

Joanne Keller
Seattle, WA

No pork dinner is complete without sauerkraut on the side.

1 onion, chopped
2 T. bacon drippings
1/4 t. caraway seed
3/4 c. white wine or chicken
   broth

2 c. sauerkraut
1 potato, peeled and grated

Sauté onion in bacon drippings; add caraway seed, wine and sauerkraut. Simmer for 30 minutes. Stir in potato; simmer for an additional 30 minutes. Serves 4.

Zweibelkuchen

Caroline Capper
Circleville, OH

This is an old German recipe, revised to use refrigerated biscuits. It's called Onion Cake but really is a hot bread, quick and delicious.

2 onions, sliced and separated
    into rings
3 T. butter
12-oz. tube refrigerated
    buttermilk biscuits

1 egg, lightly beaten
1/2 t. salt
1 c. sour cream
1 t. poppy seed

Sauté onions in butter over low heat until soft; set aside. Separate the biscuits and arrange in an ungreased 8" cake pan; press together to cover bottom completely. Spoon onions over biscuits. Blend egg, sour cream and salt; spoon over onions and sprinkle with poppy seed. Bake at 375 degrees for 30 minutes. Cut into wedges and serve warm. Makes 8 servings.

Have festival fun in your own backyard…set up a table for a pie-eating or pie throwing contest and create a dunking booth using a wading pool!

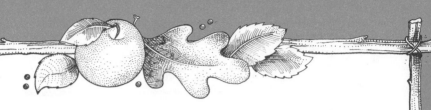

Sauerbraten

Valerie O'Reilly
Grayslake, IL

*For thicker gravy and great flavor, stir in crumbled
gingersnap cookies.*

3 to 4-lb. bottom round pot roast
2 T. oil
2 onions, chopped

2 bay leaves
1/2 c. cider vinegar
1-1/2 c. water

Brown pot roast in oil in a large heavy pot with a lid. Add remaining
ingredients; bring to a rolling boil, reduce heat and simmer 2 to
3 hours or until tender, turning meat about 4 times during cooking.
Remove and discard bay leaves before serving. Makes 6 to 8 servings.

Thinking of hosting an Oktoberfest party? Make the
invitations clever by using a photo, postcard or
map of Germany.

148

Oktoberfest

Spaetzle

Helen Fritz
Escanaba, MI

In Germany, spaetzle is served as a side dish much like potatoes or rice. The cooked spaetzle can also be pan-fried with a little butter and onions...a good leftover idea!

1 c. milk
2-1/2 c. all-purpose flour
2 eggs
2 t. salt, divided

6 c. water
1/4 c. butter
1/2 c. bread crumbs

Gradually add milk to flour, stirring until smooth. Add one egg at a time, blending after each addition. Stir in one teaspoon salt; mix well. Bring water to a boil in a saucepan and add remaining salt. Use a spoon to push dough through a colander into boiling water; boil for 5 minutes. Drain in a colander. Melt butter in a small skillet; stir in bread crumbs until browned and sprinkle over drained spaetzle. Makes 4 to 6 servings.

Stop by the local travel agency to see about buying travel posters of Germany...a simple decorating idea. Pick up blue and white balloons too; these are the colors of Munich.

German Dish

Paula Trickett
Emmaus, PA

This unique family recipe was taught to my mother 60 years ago by her Russian immigrant mother-in-law, who had learned it from a German immigrant neighbor. Since neither lady spoke English, the name was incomprehensible to my grandmother. It became known simply as "German Dish." It is such a family favorite that whenever anyone makes a big pot of German Dish, everyone is invited to come over and share.

1 lb. bacon, crisply cooked and
    crumbled, drippings reserved
10-3/4 oz. can cream of tomato
    soup
6-oz. can tomato paste
16-oz. can pork & beans

1-1/2 c. water
16-oz. pkg. prepared elbow
    macaroni
salt and pepper to taste
Garnish: grated Parmesan
    cheese

Combine bacon, 2 tablespoons reserved drippings, tomato soup, tomato paste, pork & beans and water in a Dutch oven. Simmer 7 to 10 minutes until blended, stir in macaroni and heat through. Ladle into soup bowl; sprinkle with Parmesan cheese. Makes 6 servings.

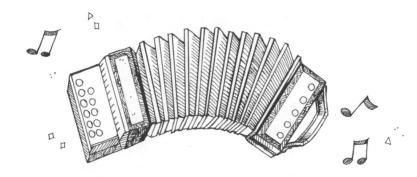

For silly fun the kids will love, play musical
chairs with polka music!

Bavarian-Style Potatoes

Kerry Mayer
Dunham Springs, LA

*The addition of eggs on top makes this potato dish
anything but plain.*

6 slices bacon, crisply cooked
    and crumbled, drippings
    reserved
1 green pepper, diced
1 onion, chopped

3 potatoes, peeled, boiled and
    diced
salt and pepper to taste
1/2 c. shredded Cheddar cheese
6 eggs

Combine bacon, 3 tablespoons reserved drippings, green pepper and
onion in a skillet. Heat and stir until golden brown, about 5 minutes.
Salt and pepper to taste. Gently toss cheese and potatoes together; stir
into bacon mixture. Break eggs over mixture, one at a time. Cook over
low heat until eggs are set; serve immediately. Serves 6.

Fun facts…until only recently, Germans traditionally ate
5 meals a day. Second breakfast consisted of coffee and
pastries, while sausage and cheese dishes filled in after lunch
and before dinner.

Pork Chops & Sauerkraut

Debbi Silvestri
Marlboro, NJ

Try substituting apple cider if you don't have apple juice on hand.

2 T. oil
4 pork chops
2 cloves garlic, minced
1 sweet onion, thinly sliced

16-oz. bag sauerkraut
1 t. caraway seed
4 T. apple juice
salt and pepper to taste

Heat oil in a large skillet over medium heat. Brown pork chops on both sides; remove from skillet and set aside. Add remaining ingredients to the skillet; sauté for 3 to 4 minutes. Arrange pork chops on top of sauerkraut mixture; cover and simmer until meat is fork tender, 30 to 45 minutes. Makes 4 servings.

Applesauce

Carol Burgess
Woodway, TX

For a change, try serving applesauce warm sprinkled with cinnamon.

4 c. MacIntosh apples, cored,
    peeled and quartered
1 c. water
1/2 c. sugar

1 t. lemon juice
1/2 t. cinnamon
1/8 t. salt

Combine apples and water in a heavy saucepan; cook over low heat, covered, until apples are very soft. Remove from heat; stir in remaining ingredients. Serve warm or cold. Makes 4 to 6 servings.

Oktoberfest

German Potato Pancakes

Laura Fuller
Fort Wayne, IN

These are yummy spread with cranberry sauce too!

2 eggs
2 T. all-purpose flour
1/4 t. baking powder
1/2 t. salt
1/4 t. pepper
6 potatoes, peeled and shredded

1/2 c. onion, finely chopped
1/4 c. oil
Garnish: applesauce, sour cream
or jam

Blend together eggs, flour, baking powder, salt and pepper in a large bowl. Stir in potatoes and onion; set aside. Heat oil in a large skillet over medium heat. In batches, drop heaping tablespoonfuls of potato mixture into the skillet. Press to flatten and cook about 3 minutes on each side, until crisp and golden. Drain on paper towels. Makes 6 servings.

Borrow tapes or compact discs from the library of brass bands and of course, oompah music to really set a festive Oktoberfest atmosphere!

Grilled Brats in Beer

Michelle Campen
Peoria, IL

These are a snap to make when cooked on the grill!

1/2 c. butter
1 onion, thinly sliced and sepa-
    rated into rings

12-oz. can beer
16-oz. pkg. bratwurst
hot dog buns

Melt butter in saucepan; add onion and heat until tender. Stir in beer. Heat bratwurst for 20 to 25 minutes on a charcoal grill 3 to 4 inches from coals, turning occasionally, until cooked through. To serve, place in buns and spoon sauce over. Serves 5 to 6.

Toss in a few onion slices when boiling bratwurst…they'll add a delicious flavor!

Pretzel Bread

Sharon Demers
Dolores, CO

A friend, whose family is German, gave me this traditional German recipe. I think it's perfect served with a good hearty soup.

1 pkg. active dry yeast
1-1/2 c. lukewarm water
1 T. sugar
1 t. salt

3 to 4 c. all-purpose flour
1 egg, beaten
Garnish: coarse salt

Dissolve yeast in water; add sugar and salt. Add flour 1/2 cup at a time, mix dough and knead. Shape into pretzel shapes, rolls or a braided loaf and place on greased baking sheet. Brush with egg and sprinkle with coarse salt. Bake at 450 degrees about 12 minutes for pretzels and rolls; 25 to 30 minutes for bread. Makes 24 servings.

Creamy Mustard Dip

Penny Sherman
Cumming, GA

A great dipper for pretzels!

8-oz. container sour cream
2 t. mustard

1/2 t. onion salt

Combine ingredients in a small bowl; stir well and chill 30 minutes. Makes about one cup.

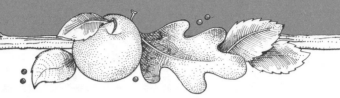

Oktoberfest Skillet

Jen Dorsey
Irvine, CA

A delicious recipe that's oh-so easy to make.

16-oz. pkg. Kielbasa, sliced
2 onions, quartered
2 tart apples, sliced

1 green pepper, sliced
2 T. butter
1/4 c. brown sugar, packed

Place sausage in skillet sprayed with non-stick vegetable spray; heat until browned around edges. Add onion, apples and pepper; heat until tender. Add butter and brown sugar; stir until mixture coats sausage and vegetables. Makes 4 servings.

Get the kids crafting to celebrate Oktoberfest. Girls will like making a blue and white ribbon hairbow, while the boys can make paper Alpine hats.

Spicy Red Potato Salad

Gladys Kielar
Perrysburg, OH

I always bring this dish to our family celebrations.

1/4 c. mayonnaise
1/4 c. fresh parsley, finely
    chopped
1/4 c. red onion, finely chopped
1/4 c. red pepper, chopped
1 t. hot pepper sauce

2 t. Dijon mustard
1 t. vinegar
1/4 t. salt
1/4 t. sugar
2 lbs. redskin potatoes, cooked
    and cut into 1/2-inch cubes

Mix all ingredients, stirring in potatoes last. Cover and chill. For a spicier taste, add more hot pepper sauce. Makes 6 to 8 servings.

Hot Cabbage Slaw

Rose Marie Benecke
Glencoe, MO

My favorite recipe because it's an old German dish my mother always made. I remember she'd always ask me to taste the dressing to be sure it was the right blend of sweet and sour.

2 T. butter
2 eggs, slightly beaten
1/4 c. white vinegar
1/2 c. milk
2 T. sugar

1/4 t. dry mustard
1/2 t. salt
1/8 t. paprika
1/8 t. pepper
5 c. cabbage, shredded

Mix all ingredients except cabbage together in a deep pan or skillet. Cook over low heat until slightly thickened, stirring constantly. Add cabbage. Heat through, but do not cook. Serve immediately. Serves 6.

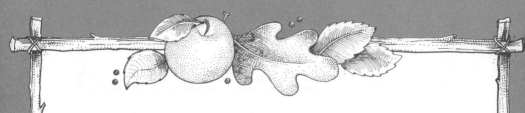

Aunt Pauline's Kraut Runza

Tracy Kelly
Lenexa, KS

Our family has made Kraut Runza for years...it's a delicious tradition! Aunt Pauline always prepared it with a "pinch of this, a dash of that" but we've successfully captured her recipe.

6 T. butter
4 eggs
3 c. milk
3-1/2 t. salt

3 c. all-purpose flour, sifted
2 pkgs. active dry yeast
1/2 c. warm water

Mix together butter, eggs, milk and salt; stir in flour. Sprinkle yeast into warm water in a small bowl; set aside until foamy. Stir yeast into flour mixture; blend. Coat hands with flour and work dough until smooth. Let rise in a warm place one hour. Roll out dough and cut into squares; fill half of each square with ground beef filling, fold into triangles and pinch edges to seal. Place on a greased baking sheet; bake 20 minutes at 375 degrees, until golden brown. Serves 4.

Ground Beef Filling:

1 lb. ground beef
3 onions, chopped
1/2 head cabbage, shredded

salt to taste
1 t. pepper or more, to taste

Brown beef with onion in skillet; set aside. Place cabbage in another skillet; add enough water to cover bottom of skillet, cover and steam until tender. Combine beef and cabbage; add salt and pepper and simmer until liquid is reduced.

Tante Midge's Red Cabbage

Theresa Gollhofer
Herndon, VA

The spices in this recipe will fill your home with a wonderful aroma.

2 T. bacon fat
1 head red cabbage, shredded
3 apples, cored, peeled and diced
1 onion, chopped
1 bay leaf
1/4 t. ground cloves
1 t. salt

2 T. brown sugar, packed
1/4 t. pepper
1/4 t. allspice
1/4 c. red wine vinegar
1/2 c. dry red wine
1/4 c. water

Melt fat in a 3-quart stockpot; layer 1/3 of the cabbage, onion and apples. Repeat for 2 more layers; set aside. Mix bay leaf, cloves, salt, brown sugar, pepper and allspice; sprinkle over cabbage layers. Combine remaining ingredients; pour over cabbage. Cook on low heat for 1-1/2 to 2 hours. Remove and discard bay leaf. Serves 6 to 8.

For an outdoor Oktoberfest celebration, set up a tent in the backyard with large tables and chairs. Invite the men to sport suspenders and the women to wear white aprons...just in keeping with the festive mood!

German Apple Cake

Debi DeVore
Dover, OH

A nice moist cake. One bite, and you'll be hooked!

3 eggs
2 c. sugar
1 c. oil
1 t. vanilla extract
2 c. all-purpose flour
2 t. cinnamon

1 t. baking soda
1/2 t. salt
4 tart apples, cored, peeled and
    chopped
3/4 c. chopped pecans

Blend eggs, sugar, oil and vanilla in a mixing bowl. In a second bowl, combine flour, cinnamon, baking soda and salt; add to egg mixture, mixing well. Fold in apples and pecans. Pour into a greased 13"x9" baking pan. Bake at 350 degrees for 55 to 60 minutes or until a toothpick inserted near the center comes out clean. Cool pan on a wire rack. Spread frosting over cake. Makes 12 to 16 servings.

Frosting:

8-oz. pkg. cream cheese,
    softened
2 T. butter, softened

2 c. powdered sugar

Blend together cream cheese and butter. Stir in powdered sugar and blend until smooth.

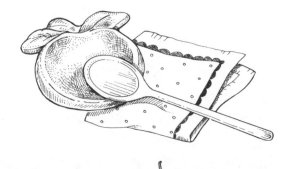

Noodle & Cheese Kugel

Cathy Hillier
Salt Lake City, UT

Try this quick and reliable recipe any night of the week.

8-oz. pkg. cooked wide egg
    noodles
4 eggs
2 c. milk, heated
8-oz. pkg. cream cheese,
    softened

2 T. sugar
1/2 c. butter, softened
salt to taste

Combine all ingredients in a large mixing bowl; stir well. Spread into a greased 13"x9" baking dish. Bake at 375 degrees for one hour. Let cool for 15 minutes; cut into 2-inch squares to serve. Makes 6 to 8 servings.

Give kazoos as party favors, then everyone can play along with the music.

German Chocolate Brownies

Lois Bohm
Clark, NJ

I made these brownies for my husband on our first Valentine's Day.
I've made them every year since.

14-oz. pkg. caramels,
   unwrapped
5-oz. can evaporated milk,
   divided
18-1/4 oz. pkg. German
   chocolate cake mix

1 c. chopped nuts
3/4 c. butter, melted
1 to 2 c. semi-sweet chocolate
   chips

Melt caramels with 1/3 cup evaporated milk in a double boiler; reduce heat and keep warm. Combine cake mix, nuts and butter in a mixing bowl; stir until mixture holds together. Press half the cake mixture into a greased and floured 13"x9" baking pan. Bake at 350 degrees for 6 minutes; remove from oven. Sprinkle chocolate chips over hot crust; spread melted caramels on top. Crumble remaining cake mixture on top. Bake at 350 degrees for 15 to 18 additional minutes. Cool; cut into bars. Makes one dozen.

German beer steins make terrific flower vases filled with the bold colors of calendula or dahlias...ideal for a buffet table.

Oktoberfest

Blueberry Kuchen

Nonnie Arndt
Chili, WI

Spoon into custard cups and top with a bit of cream.

1-1/2 c. all-purpose flour
3/4 c. sugar
2 t. baking powder
1-1/2 t. lemon zest
1/2 t. nutmeg
1/4 t. salt

2/3 c. milk
1/4 c. butter, melted
1 egg, beaten
1 t. vanilla extract
2 c. blueberries

Combine flour, sugar, baking powder, lemon zest, nutmeg and salt; stir in milk, butter, egg and vanilla. Beat until well blended. Pour into a greased 13"x9" baking pan. Sprinkle with blueberries and topping. Bake at 350 degrees for 40 minutes. Makes about 24 servings.

Topping:

3/4 c. sugar
1/2 c. all-purpose flour

1/4 c. butter, melted

Combine ingredients in small bowl; toss with a fork until crumbly.

Autumn is the mellower season, and what we lose in flowers
we more than gain in fruits.

-Samuel Butler

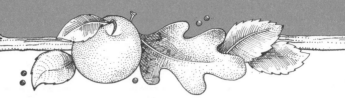

Apple Strudel

Connie Magee
Dagsboro, DE

You can substitute peaches if you prefer...just as tasty!

8 apples, peeled, cored and
   sliced
cinnamon-sugar to taste
1/2 c. butter
1 c. sugar

1 t. baking powder
1 c. all-purpose flour
1/2 t. salt
1 egg

Place a thick layer of apples in a buttered 13"x9" baking dish. Sprinkle with cinnamon-sugar; dot with butter. Mix together sugar, baking powder, flour, salt and egg until crumbly; sprinkle over apples and bake at 350 degrees until golden. Serves 16 to 20.

Don't forget to take pictures and remember the camcorder to capture the kids dancing the polka and marching in the all-kazoo band.

Spider Pizza

Deborah Biondo
Slingerlands, NY

A family tradition...I make this pizza each Friday the 13th throughout the year, and of course on Halloween.

1 pkg. active dry yeast
1 c. warm water
1 t. sugar
1-1/2 t. salt
2 T. oil
2 c. all-purpose flour
28-oz. can crushed tomatoes
1 T. dried oregano
1 t. dried basil
2 cloves garlic, minced
1 c. shredded mozzarella cheese
6-oz. can whole black olives, drained

Dissolve yeast in water; stir in sugar, salt and oil. Stir in flour; let rise for 30 to 40 minutes. Spread dough out on a greased 12" pizza pan; set aside. Combine tomatoes, oregano, basil and garlic; spread over dough. Sprinkle with cheese; set aside. To make spider bodies, slice half the olives lengthwise; arrange on the sauce mixture. Cut remaining olives in 8 lengthwise slices; arrange 4 slices on each side of each half to make a spider with legs. Bake at 450 degrees for 20 minutes. Serves 4.

Little ones will love playing spooky Tic-Tac-Toe! Just cut a board from black cardstock and divide into 9 squares using glued-in-place ribbon. Cut-outs of ghosts and pumpkins make great game pieces.

Bubblin' Berry Brew
Jo Ann

Guests will find an eerie fake hand floating in this punch!

disposable plastic glove
10-oz. pkg. frozen raspberries,
  thawed
2-1/2 c. cranberry juice
2 .25-oz. envs. unflavored
  gelatin mix

2 ltrs. ginger ale
2 ltrs. non-alcoholic sparkling
  apple cider

Wash and rinse glove; set aside. Combine raspberries and cranberry juice. Pour 2 cups of the mixture into a small saucepan; sprinkle with gelatin and let stand 2 minutes. Warm mixture over low heat, stirring until gelatin dissolves; blend back into first raspberry mixture. Carefully pour into inverted glove; gather top of glove together and secure with a rubber band. Freeze until solid. At serving time, combine ginger ale and sparkling cider in a punch bowl. Remove frozen "hand" from freezer, dip into warm water just long enough to easily remove plastic glove; float in punch bowl. Makes 16 servings.

Turn your front yard into an eerie graveyard by filling it with "gravestones." Cut pieces of Styrofoam® into shapes and paint with watered-down gray acrylic paint; let dry. Use a pen to add words on the "gravestone." To secure, insert two, 6-inch bamboo stakes into the bottom of each "gravestone," turn upright and gently press into the ground.

Doggie Bones

Liz Hall
Worthington, IN

*Give the kids a giggle when you tell them you're serving up
some graveyard grub!*

1 lb. bacon   8-oz. pkg. pretzel rods

Roll bacon spiral fashion around each pretzel rod. Arrange 10 rods on
a paper towel-covered microwaveable plate; cover with another paper
towel and microwave on high for 6 minutes or until bacon is crisp.
Repeat with remaining pretzel rods and bacon. Serves 4.

Knucklebones

Michelle Campen
Peoria, IL

This is really toasted ravioli, but it's all in the name!

2 T. milk   oil for deep-frying
1 egg   Garnish: spaghetti sauce, grated
1-lb. pkg. frozen ravioli, thawed   Parmesan cheese
2/3 to 1 c. seasoned bread
    crumbs

Beat milk and egg together; dip ravioli in mixture and coat with bread
crumbs. Heat 1/2-inch depth oil in skillet; heat ravioli on each side
until golden and drain. Sprinkle with Parmesan cheese. Serve with
warm spaghetti sauce and extra Parmesan cheese. Makes 12 to 14.

This year, try handing out goodies other than
sweets...glow-in-the-dark yo-yo's, rubber
stamps, stickers, bendy skeletons,
ghoulish rubber balls and
eyeball erasers are still lots of fun
long after the candy's gone.

Frightfully Fun Halloween

Eyeballs

Robin Wilson
Altamonte Springs, FL

Drizzle catsup over "eyes" to make them look a little bloodshot!

12 hard-boiled eggs, cut in
  halves
1/2 c. Thousand Island salad
  dressing

salt and pepper to taste
Garnish: paprika

Arrange egg white halves on a serving plate. Mash egg yolks and stir
in salad dressing. Add salt and pepper to taste; spoon into egg white
halves. Sprinkle with paprika; chill. Makes 2 dozen.

Spicy Bat Wings

Ziggy Shenefiel
Oakton, VA

So devilishly delightful!

3 lbs. chicken wings
12-oz. can cola

12-oz. bottle catsup

Spray 13"x9" baking pan with non-stick vegetable spray. Arrange
wings in pan, cover with aluminum foil, and bake at 425 degrees for
45 minutes or until tender. Remove from oven. Mix cola and catsup;
spoon over wings. Bake uncovered for an additional 45 minutes,
basting occasionally. Makes about 2-1/2 dozen.

For a hauntingly good Halloween buffet, decorate with dried
leaves and dead flowers sprinkled on the table. A bouquet of
red roses, that turn black when dried, is particularly ghoulish!

Frosted "Snails"

Mary Bateman
Lykens, PA

No, not really snails...gotcha!

1 pkg. active dry yeast
1/4 c. warm water
1 c. milk
1/4 c. butter
1/2 c. sugar
1 t. salt

5 c. all-purpose flour
3 eggs, beaten and divided
1 t. lemon zest
1 egg, slightly beaten
Garnish: frosting, chopped nuts

Dissolve yeast in warm water; set aside. Scald milk; add butter, sugar and salt. Cool to lukewarm. Add enough flour to make a thick batter; mix in yeast mixture, 2 eggs and lemon zest and stir well. Add enough flour to make a soft dough. Turn out on lightly floured surface; knead until satiny. Place in greased bowl; cover and let rise until double in bulk. Pinch off a portion; roll into a rope 15 inches long and 1/2 inch thick. Starting at center, roll into a spiral. Place on a greased baking sheet; repeat with remaining dough. Brush with reserved beaten egg and let rise until double again. Bake at 375 degrees for 15 to 20 minutes until golden. When cool, decorate with frosting and nuts. Makes 2 dozen.

Let the kids, or adults, plunge their hands into buckets filled with frightening foods and then let them guess what's inside...coat everything lightly with oil for an extra-slimy feel! Tell them pumpkin seeds are fingernails, rawhide dog bones are human bones, and peeled grapes or small boiled eggs are eyeballs!

Frightfully Delicious Dip

Marsha Brown
Tulsa, OK

Serve with a basket of crackers or toasted pita crisps.

14-oz. can artichoke hearts,
   drained and quartered
1-1/2 oz. pkg. garlic-flavored
   soup mix

1 c. shredded Swiss cheese
1 c. mayonnaise
1 c. sour cream

Mix all ingredients together; spread in a greased 13"x9" baking pan.
Bake at 350 degrees for 30 minutes. Makes about 4 cups.

Witches' Hats

Liz Wernsing
Teutopolis, IL

Even little goblins can help make this easy-to-fix snack.

12-oz. jar pasteurized processed
   cheese sauce

round buttery crackers
cone-shaped corn snacks

Squeeze a one-inch circle of cheese in center of each cracker; top with
a corn snack. Makes as many as you like!

Set the scene for a mad scientist's lab…fill gallon-size
apothecary jars with water that's been tinted
green with food coloring, then have fun!
A head of cauliflower looks like a brain,
olive slices frozen in ice cubes resemble
eyeballs, drop in a plastic skull or even
glow-in-the-dark bugs.

Mini Mummies

*Tina Stidam
Delaware, OH*

*Leave part of the sausage peeking out and place dots of mustard and
poppy seeds for eyes! Terrific with full-size sausages too!*

2 8-oz. tubes refrigerated
    crescent rolls
16-oz. pkg. cocktail sausages

Garnish: mustard, catsup

Separate crescent dough into 4 rectangles; roll each out to 1/8-inch
thickness. Cut each into six, 3-inch long strips; roll a sausage in each
strip. Arrange seam side-down on an ungreased baking sheet; bake at
375 degrees for 10 to 12 minutes. Serve with mustard and catsup.
Makes 4 dozen.

Create a trail of glowing pumpkins in no time…after
carving, tuck two strings of outdoor-safe
electric lights inside each pumpkin. Hide any
utility cords with mulch.

Eyes of Newt

*Geri Peterson
Pleasanton, CA*

Spoon on some extra cream cheese and top with an olive-stuffed pimento slice to make these tasty roll-ups look like eyes!

2 c. sour cream
8-oz. pkg. cream cheese,
  softened
4-oz. can diced jalapeños,
  drained and divided

2 4-oz. cans diced green chiles
6-oz. can roasted peanuts,
  chopped
5 to 6 12-inch flour tortillas
Garnish: picante sauce

Combine sour cream, cream cheese, half the jalapeños, chiles and peanuts; spread on tortillas. Reserve remaining jalapeños for another recipe. Roll up tortillas; cover with plastic wrap and refrigerate for 8 hours. Slice; serve with picante sauce. Makes about 5 dozen.

Drive guests batty…cut out flying bats from sheets of black adhesive shelf liner. They easily adhere to mirrors or windows and remove in a snap; just peel them right off.

Murky Water

SueMary Burford-Smith
Tulsa, OK

Fun to sip served from old canning jars.

3 qts. water
3 c. sugar
1 pt. brewed tea
3-oz. can frozen orange juice
   concentrate

3-oz. can frozen lemonade
   concentrate
3-oz. can frozen grape juice
   concentrate
2 ltrs. lemon-lime soda, chilled

Combine water and sugar in a saucepan. Bring to a boil; reduce heat and simmer for 8 minutes. Cool to room temperature. Combine tea and concentrates; add sugar mixture. Add lemon-lime soda just before serving. Makes about 3 gallons.

Paint the perfect spiderweb punch bowl for serving up magical potions. Wash and dry a glass punch bowl, then apply a thick layer of etching cream to the outside; let sit 5 minutes. Remove cream with water and a soft cloth. Use black glass paint to create a spiderweb on the outside of the bowl. Let dry for 10 days before hand-washing.

Devilishly Delightful Dip

Susan Biffignani
Fenton, MO

Toss a few gummy worms on top!

1 c. sour cream
4-1/2 oz. can deviled ham
1 T. plus 1-1/2 t. onion, minced

1 t. mustard
1/8 t. pepper

Mix all ingredients together; cover. Refrigerate for at least one hour.
Makes 1-1/2 cups.

Serve up beverages every goblin will love. Drop a scoop of
vanilla ice cream into a glass of root beer and call it "A Ghost
in a Graveyard"...irresistible to kids when sipped through a
black licorice "straw."

Mud Pie

Heather Cipriani
Pittsburgh, PA

Keep the mud pie joke going...don't use a pretty pie server, serve this to guests using a new trowel!

1/2 pkg. chocolate wafers
1/2 c. butter, melted
1 qt. coffee-flavored ice cream,
   softened

1-1/2 c. fudge sauce
Garnish: whipped topping and
   slivered almonds

Crush wafers and add butter; mix well. Press into a 9" pie plate. Spread with ice cream; place in freezer until ice cream is firm. Top with fudge sauce; freeze for approximately 10 hours. Slice pie into 8 wedges and serve on chilled dessert plates. Top each wedge with whipped topping and slivered almonds before serving. Makes 8 servings.

For a shimmering pumpkin, coat it in spray adhesive and quickly sprinkle with clear glitter...sparkly!!

Buggy Cupcakes

Jackie Crough
Salina, KS

Top each cupcake with white frosting, then add a "bug!" Arrange 2 black jellybeans to make a spider head and body, then add 1-1/2 inch lengths of black licorice whip candy for the legs.

18-1/4 oz. pkg. German
   chocolate cake mix
8-oz. pkg. cream cheese,
   softened
1/3 c. sugar

1 egg
1/4 c. oil
1 c. semi-sweet chocolate chips
Garnish: frosting

Prepare cake mix according to package directions; set aside. In a separate bowl, combine cream cheese, sugar, egg, oil and chocolate chips; spoon one rounded teaspoon of filling in center of each paper-lined mini muffin cup. Fill muffin cups 2/3 full with cake mixture. Bake at 350 degrees for 15 to 20 minutes. Cool and frost as desired. Makes about 2 dozen.

Dress up a mantel with a Halloween village…distress painted wooden houses with sandpaper, add some creepy "cobwebs" and toy winged creatures of all kinds…bats, owls and crows are particularly eerie.

Black Cat Cookies

Julie Merkel
Evansville, IN

Friendly little felines!

1/2 c. butter, softened
3/4 c. sugar
1 egg
3/4 t. vanilla extract
2 c. all-purpose flour
1/2 t. baking soda

1/2 t. salt
Garnish: white frosting, black
food coloring, green, orange
and yellow candy-coated
chocolates, and red licorice
whip candy

Cream butter and sugar in a medium mixing bowl until light and fluffy.
Add egg and vanilla, mixing well; set aside. Combine flour, baking
soda and salt; add to creamed mixture. Divide dough into thirds; roll
out onto lightly floured wax paper. Cut with cookie cutters as desired
and arrange on lightly greased baking sheets. Bake at 375 degrees for
10 to 12 minutes; set aside to cool. Combine white frosting with black
food coloring until the desired color is achieved. Place green or orange
candies in frosting for "eyes" and use a yellow one for each cat's
"nose." Add lengths of red licorice whip for "whiskers." Makes about
2-1/2 dozen.

Windows filled with spooky bird silhouettes make any home
look like a haunted birdcage! Cut flocks of crows from black
plastic film and simply smooth in place to adhere to windows.

Hauntingly Good Haystacks

Kim Rosenbalm
Hamilton, OH

With only 2 ingredients, it's a can't-miss snack.

2 c. butterscotch chips

5-oz. can chow mein noodles

Melt chips in a saucepan over low heat. Remove from heat; stir in noodles to coat. Drop by tablespoonfuls onto waxed paper; cool. Makes 2 dozen.

Spooky Spiders

JoEllen Johnson
Beaver, OH

Great "insects" for the kids' Halloween party!

creamy peanut butter
buttery round crackers

pretzel sticks
raisins

For each spider, spread peanut butter on a cracker, place 4 pretzel sticks on each side for "legs," spread peanut butter on a second cracker and press together gently. Use a little peanut butter to stick 2 raisin "eyes" to top cracker. Make as many as you like!

Creepy laughter, crashing thunder, rattling chains…don't forget to pick up a CD or tape of scary sounds.

Monster Eyes

Michelle Urdahl
Litchfield, MN

Oh-so simple bewitching bites...just spread each bagel half with sour cream mixture and place a black olive half in the center. Eek!

2 c. mayonnaise
2 c. sour cream
1 T. seasoned salt flavor
   enhancer
1 T. dill weed

1 onion, diced
2 2.5-oz. pkgs. deli corned beef,
   chopped
mini bagels, split
Garnish: black olives, halved

Mix together all ingredients except bagels; chill one hour before serving. Spread on bagel halves. Makes about 4-1/2 cups.

Serve a bowl of soup that stares back! Scoop the centers from mini mozzarella balls, fill with sliced pimento-stuffed olives and float in any favorite soup...it's eye popping!

Sloppy Goblins

Lynda Robson
Boston, MA

Let the kids create their own goblin "face" for a howling good time!

3 c. celery, chopped
1 c. onions, chopped
1 c. catsup
1 c. barbecue sauce
1 c. water
2 T. vinegar
2 T. Worcestershire sauce
2 T. brown sugar, packed
1 t. chili powder

1 t. salt
1 t. pepper
1/2 t. garlic powder
3 to 4-lb. boneless chuck roast
14 to 18 hamburger buns
Garnish: banana peppers, sliced
    olives, carrot crinkles, pretzel
    sticks, sliced pimentos, fresh
    parsley sprigs

Combine the first 12 ingredients; in a slow cooker; mix well. Add roast; cover and cook on high setting 6 to 7 hours or until tender. Remove roast; shred meat, return to slow cooker and heat through. Serve on hamburger buns. Makes 14 to 18 servings.

Deliver creepy party invitations…add plastic bugs to floral tubes; top each with a cork. Tie a tea-stained paper mailing tag on each "specimen" tube giving all the party details.

Monster Claws

Mary Murray
Gooseberry Patch

A haunted hint...serve dipping sauces in small plastic cauldrons or Jack-'O-Lanterns.

2 T. all-purpose flour
1 T. plus 2 t. Cajun seasoning, divided
1 lb. boneless, skinless chicken breasts, cut into strips
1-1/2 c. corn flake cereal, crushed
2 T. green onion, chopped
3 eggs, beaten
1 red pepper, cut in triangles
Garnish: favorite dipping sauces

Combine flour and 2 teaspoons Cajun seasoning in a plastic zipping bag; add chicken, shaking bag to coat. Mix cereal crumbs, green onion and remaining seasoning in a shallow bowl; set aside. Place eggs in a bowl; dip each chicken strip, then coat with crumb mixture. Arrange on a lightly greased baking sheet. Bake at 350 degrees for 10 minutes; set aside to cool slightly. Cut a slit in the end of each strip; slide a pepper triangle inside slit to form "claw nails." Makes about 2-1/2 dozen.

For an eerie effect, hang glow-in-the-dark bats, skeletons and spiders from the ceilings and trees. Try using colored chalk to write Halloween messages along the walkway...a black light will enhance the frightful effect!

Get Lost Vampire Dressing

Gail Prather
Bethel, MN

A bit of garlic will make any vampire shoo!

1/4 c. red wine vinegar
1/4 c. oil
1-1/2 c. mayonnaise

1 t. minced garlic
1/8 t. pepper
1/4 c. powdered sugar

Combine all ingredients in a blender; blend for one minute. Refrigerate for at least one hour. Makes about 2 cups.

Armadillo Eggs

Rita Morgan
Pueblo, CO

These cheese-stuffed biscuits will have guests howling for more!

16-oz. jar whole jalapeños, drained, seeded and sliced lengthwise
2 c. shredded Cheddar cheese

1 lb. ground pork sausage
2 10-oz. cans refrigerated biscuit dough

Stuff jalapeños with cheese. Divide sausage into small balls; press into thin strips. Place a stuffed jalapeño onto each sausage strip; roll jalapeño in the sausage, pressing firmly. Place wrapped jalapeños on a greased baking pan and bake 40 to 50 minutes at 350 degrees until sausage is browned. Remove from oven; allow to cool 10 minutes. Wrap one jalapeño roll in each biscuit; bake at 350 degrees 10 to 12 minutes until golden. Makes 16.

In masks and gowns we haunt the street
And knock on doors for trick or treat.
Tonight we are the king and queen,
For oh tonight it's Halloween!

-Jack Prelutsky

Fungus Salad

Flo Burtnett
Gage, OK

*Well, technically mushrooms ARE a fungus! But don't let that stop
you from enjoying this yummy Greek salad!*

16-oz. pkg. sliced mushrooms
1/2 c. green onions, chopped
8-oz. pkg. shredded Cheddar
   cheese
1/4 c. oil

1/8 c. red wine vinegar
1/2 T. sugar
1-1/2 t. Greek seasoning

Combine mushrooms, onion and cheese in a serving bowl; cover and
refrigerate. Mix together oil, vinegar, sugar and seasoning; pour
mixture over mushrooms before serving. Makes 8 to 10 servings.

Small glow sticks give off an eerie greenish glow...perfect
for Halloween! Tie several to string that's been attached to
helium balloons. Let them sail throughout your house to
create spooky floating lights.

Squirmy Salad

Michele Hicks
Bunker Hill, MN

This spaghetti salad is simply delicious.

16-oz. pkg. spaghetti, prepared
2 tomatoes, diced
1 green pepper, diced
1 onion, diced

1 cucumber, peeled and diced
16-oz. bottle creamy Italian
   salad dressing
2.75-oz. jar salad seasoning

Mix all ingredients together in a large serving bowl; refrigerate overnight. Serves 10 to 12.

Have a Halloween film festival every weekend in October.
Check out the library or video store for old classics or even a
newer horror movie, then pop some popcorn and invite
friends over!

Monkey Paws

Deborah Ellis
Fair Grove, MO

Gotcha! No monkeys were harmed in the making of this recipe.

3 12-oz. tubes refrigerated
   biscuits
3/4 c. sugar
1/2 t. cinnamon

1/4 c. evaporated milk
1/2 c. brown sugar, packed
3/4 c. butter

Cut biscuits into quarters; coat with sugar and cinnamon. Stack biscuits in a greased Bundt® pan; set aside. In a small saucepan, bring milk, brown sugar and butter to a boil until thick; pour over biscuits. Bake at 350 degrees for 35 minutes. Cool slightly, then remove from pan. Serve warm. Makes 12 to 15 servings.

Create a creepy "mist" that drifts out of a carved pumpkin face. Just place a can inside a large carved pumpkin, then fill the can halfway with hot water. Wearing gloves, gently drop dry ice into water.

Golden Tombstones

Roxanne Bixby
West Franklin, NH

Drizzle with a little maple syrup for a breakfast treat.

1-1/2 c. all-purpose flour	2/3 c. margarine, melted
1/2 c. raisins	1 T. baking powder
1-1/2 c. quick-cooking oats, uncooked	1/2 t. salt
	1/3 c. milk
1/2 c. chopped walnuts	1 egg
1/4 c. sugar	

Combine flour, raisins, oats, walnuts and sugar; mix in margarine, baking powder, salt, milk and egg. On a floured surface, pat dough into a 12"x9" rectangle. Cut into twelve, 3-inch squares, then cut each square in half diagonally. Place on an ungreased baking sheet; bake at 425 degrees for 10 to 12 minutes. Makes 2 dozen.

White Lumina pumpkins are especially pretty. For something different, use a 1/4-inch drill bit to drill holes in a hollowed-out pumpkin shell, then slip battery operated white lights through each drilled opening...lovely!

Spiderweb Soup

Lynnette Zeigler
South Lake Tahoe, CA

Instead of a dollop of sour cream, create a spiderweb in each bowl!
Spoon sour cream into a plastic zipping bag; seal bag. Snip off one
corner and pipe sour cream in circles over individual servings of soup.
Run the tip of a knife through the sour cream to make a "spiderweb."

1 c. red onion, chopped
1 red pepper, chopped
2 cloves garlic, minced
2 boneless, skinless chicken
   breasts
1 T. oil

7 c. chicken broth
9-oz. pkg. frozen corn, thawed
1 t. dried cumin
2 c. tortilla chips, lightly crushed
1 c. shredded Cheddar cheese
Garnish: sour cream, cilantro

Sauté onion, pepper, garlic and chicken in oil for 7 to 8 minutes;
remove chicken. Pour in broth; bring to a simmer. Add corn and
cumin; cook for 10 minutes. Shred chicken; stir into soup. Place some
chips in each bowl; ladle soup over chips. Sprinkle with cheese; stir.
Garnish with dollops of sour cream and sprinkle with cilantro. Serves
6 to 8.

Hand out the ultimate caramel apple instead of candy.
Little trick-or-treaters will be amazed when they see apples
coated in caramel and chopped nuts, then drizzled
in white or milk chocolate!

Ghostly White Chili

Wanda Sims
Madison, IN

Serve with some spooky tortilla chips! Using Halloween cookie cutters, cut plain tortillas, one at a time, into shapes. Lightly spray shapes with non-stick vegetable spray and place on a baking sheet. Bake at 350 degrees for 5 to 7 minutes; remove and let cool.

9 c. chicken broth
1 onion, chopped
10-oz. can diced tomatoes with chiles
4.5-oz. can chopped green chiles
2 15-oz. cans Great Northern beans

2 t. dried cumin
2 t. dried oregano
1/4 t. ground cloves
3 c. boneless, skinless chicken breasts, cooked and diced
Garnish: shredded Monterey Jack cheese, sour cream

Mix together the first 8 ingredients in a large saucepan and simmer for 1-1/2 hours. Add chicken; cook until heated through. Spoon into serving bowls; garnish with cheese and sour cream. Serves 8 to 10.

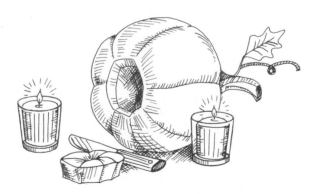

Try cutting the circle from a pumpkin in the bottom instead of around the stem when it's time to carve. Now, it's easy to set the pumpkin over a candle and the "lid" won't fall in!

Green Wonders

Dawn Psik
Aliquippa, PA

*This recipe was brought back to Pennsylvania by my mother
when she was visiting the South. They have the best flavor
and are so easy to make.*

2 10-oz. pkgs. frozen spinach,
   cooked and drained
2 c. herbed stuffing mix
2 onions, finely chopped
5 eggs, beaten

1-1/2 t. dried thyme
3/4 c. butter, melted
1/2 c. grated Parmesan cheese
2 t. garlic salt
salt and pepper to taste

Mix all ingredients and chill for 2 hours. Shape into balls, place on an
ungreased baking sheet and bake 20 to 30 minutes at 350 degrees.
Serve warm. Makes about 6 dozen.

You wouldn't believe, On All Hallow's Eve
What lots of fun we can make,
With apples to bob, And nuts on the hob,
And a ring-and-thimble cake.

–Carolyn Wells

Frog Eye Salad

Kathleen Zieroff
Saginaw, MI

I love making this salad...I've never told anyone what the "eyes" are!

3/4 c. sugar
1/2 t. all-purpose flour
1/2 t. salt
1 egg, beaten
20-oz. can chunk pineapple,
    drained and juice reserved
20-oz. can crushed pineapple,
    drained and juice reserved

1 t. lemon juice
1 c. prepared acini di pepe pasta
2 11-oz. cans mandarin
    oranges, drained
8-oz. container frozen whipped
    topping, thawed
1 c. mini marshmallows

Mix sugar, flour, salt, egg and 2/3 cup of reserved pineapple juice in a saucepan; cook until thickened. Add lemon juice; cool. Stir sugar mixture into prepared pasta; cover and chill. Add remaining ingredients; stir to coat. Chill for at least one additional hour before serving. Serves 8 to 10.

A great slumber party idea...start a ghost story circle. Sit in a circle and begin telling a scary ghost story. Each person adds to the story until it reaches a scary, surprise ending!

Halloween Pumpkin Roll

Tammy Hurt
Eau Claire, WI

*Sprinkle plastic spiders or gummy worms around the edges of the
serving plate...just for a little All Hallow's Eve surprise.*

3 eggs
1 c. sugar
2/3 c. canned pumpkin
1 t. baking soda
1/2 t. cinnamon
3/4 c. all-purpose flour

1 c. pecans or walnuts, chopped
8-oz. pkg. cream cheese,
  softened
1 c. powdered sugar
3/4 t. vanilla extract
2 T. butter

Combine eggs, sugar, pumpkin, baking soda, cinnamon and flour; mix
until smooth and set aside. Line a jelly-roll pan with wax paper
sprayed with non-stick cooking spray. Pour pumpkin mixture into pan
and sprinkle with nuts. Bake at 375 degrees for 10 to 15 minutes.
Turn onto a muslin towel that has been sprinkled with powdered
sugar. Remove wax paper; roll up cake in towel and let cool. Combine
cream cheese, powdered sugar, vanilla and butter; blend until smooth.
Unroll cooled cake and spread with cream cheese mixture. Re-roll the
cake without the towel; wrap in plastic wrap and refrigerate at least
one hour. Unwrap and slice to serve. Makes 15 to 18 servings.

To create a fragrant pumpkin, use an apple corer to carve out
round vents in a hollowed-out
pumpkin. Rub pumpkin pie spices
or cinnamon on the underside
of the pumpkin's lid, or push
cloves into it. Set a lighted
tea-light candle inside. This will
give off a wonderful scent for
about 6 hours!

TO GRANDMOTHER'S
House We Go!

Maple-Glazed Turkey

Virginia Watson
Scranton, PA

For the best taste, use only real maple syrup.

12-lb. turkey, giblet package
   removed and reserved for
   use in another recipe
favorite stuffing, if desired
4 T. butter, melted and divided
salt and pepper to taste

1 T. fresh sage, minced
1 T. fresh marjoram, minced
2 T. fresh parsley, minced
3-1/2 c. chicken broth
3 T. maple syrup
1/8 t. ground ginger

Rinse turkey and pat dry; loosely stuff if desired. Place in a large roasting pan; loosely tie legs together with kitchen string. Brush turkey with 2 tablespoons melted butter and sprinkle generously with salt and pepper. Insert meat thermometer into thickest part of thigh without touching bone. Mix together sage, thyme and parsley; loosen skin on turkey's breast and spoon half of the herb mixture under the skin. Place 1/2 cup of broth in the roasting pan. Roast for 2-1/2 hours at 325 degrees, basting every half hour with an additional 1/2 cup of broth and pan juices. Blend the remaining butter, remaining herbs, maple syrup and ginger in a small bowl; brush turkey with mixture. Continue roasting an additional 30 minutes or until meat thermometer reads 180 degrees. Allow turkey to stand about 15 minutes before slicing. Makes 10 to 12 servings.

For extra sparkle, wrap vintage beaded bracelets, the kind on stretchy string, around votives and set at each place setting.

Thanksgiving Sausage Stuffing

Karen Pilcher
Burleson, TX

Turn any extra stuffing into great finger food by rolling into 2-inch balls and baking at 400 degrees until golden.

1 t. ground sausage, browned
3/4 c. red onion, chopped
1-1/2 c. celery, chopped
1/2 c. butter
1/2 loaf sourdough bread, cubed
    (about 9 cups)
1 t. salt

1-1/2 t. dried sage
1 t. dried thyme
1/2 t. pepper
3/4 c. raisins
1 apple, cored, peeled and cubed
1 c. corn

Combine ground sausage, onion and celery in a skillet; heat until onions are tender. Stir in butter and bread; add remaining ingredients and stir to mix. Use to stuff a 12-pound turkey or 8 Cornish game hens. Makes 9 cups.

Snap up pumpkin-glazed yellowware when spotted at flea markets...beautiful for a Thanksgiving Day buffet table!

Feta & Walnut Salad

Denise Neal
Clayton, CA

*If I think my guests won't care for the tart taste of cranberries,
I just substitute cherry tomatoes.*

5-oz. pkg. mixed salad greens
3/4 c. dried cranberries
1/2 c. feta cheese, crumbled
1/2 c. chopped walnuts, toasted

2 T. balsamic vinegar
1 T. honey
1 t. Dijon mustard
1/4 c. olive oil

Toss greens, cranberries, feta cheese and walnuts together in a large bowl. In a small bowl, whisk vinegar and honey until well blended; gradually add oil, whisking until combined. Pour over salad and toss to coat. Serves 4 to 6.

For a Thanksgiving centerpiece...pile Jack-be-Little and Baby-Boo pumpkins along with Acorn and Dumpling squash on a cake stand. Simple yet so eye-catching.

Rosemary Roasted Pork Loin

Rachael Leonardis
Katy, TX

So juicy and tender...our favorite way to enjoy pork roast.

2 t. dried rosemary
2 t. dry mustard
1 t. salt
1 t. pepper

1 t. ground ginger
2 T. olive oil
6 cloves garlic, minced
3-lb. boneless pork loin

Crush together rosemary, mustard, salt, pepper and ginger in a mortar and pestle. Add oil and garlic to make a paste; set aside. Place roast in a roasting pan and rub with garlic mixture; let stand at room temperature for 30 to 45 minutes. Bake at 350 degrees for one to 1-1/2 hours. Let stand 15 to 20 minutes before slicing. Serves 3 to 4.

Break the stem off a mini pumpkin, and drill a hole in the top of each to hold a taper candle. Press the pumpkin on a candlestick's spike and add a taper.

Croissant Stuffing

Valerie Boersma
Alfred, NY

This recipe will always hold a special place in my heart. I was jotting it down to share with my sister, when halfway though writing it down, I felt a little funny and decided to finish in the morning. Little did I know that when I did finish sharing it with her, I'd be the proud new mother of an incredible baby girl. I went into labor that night and received the best Christmas present ever!

1/2 lb. bacon, cut into bite-size pieces
2 onions, chopped
2 bunches green onions, chopped
6 day-old croissants, torn into bite-size pieces (8 cups)

1 t. dried thyme
1 t. dried marjoram
1 t. dried sage
1 t. dried rosemary
salt and pepper to taste
2 to 4 T. chicken broth

Cook bacon in large skillet until crisp; remove with slotted spoon. Reserve 1/2 cup drippings in skillet. Add onions to skillet and sauté until tender; set aside. Combine bacon, croissants, herbs, salt and pepper in a large bowl; stir in onion mixture. Toss well; drizzle with chicken broth. Spoon into a greased 13"x9" baking pan; cover. Bake at 350 degrees for 30 to 35 minutes; uncover and bake for an additional 20 to 25 minutes. Makes 8 cups.

Bring the Thanksgiving hostess a bouquet of Fall flowers in a vintage glass vase...the vase is left behind as a "thank you." For a splash of holiday color, use fresh cranberries as a flower frog instead of pebbles or marbles to hold stems in place.

Corn Pudding

Janet McRoberts
Lexington, KY

An old family recipe shared with me by a dear friend.

14-3/4 oz. can creamed corn
2 eggs, lightly beaten
1 c. evaporated milk
1/4 c. sugar

2-1/2 T. all-purpose flour
2 T. butter, melted
salt to taste

Combine all ingredients; mix well. Pour into a greased 2-quart casserole dish. Bake at 325 degrees for 50 minutes to one hour; let stand 10 minutes. Serves 6.

Turn a handsome painted bench into a buffet table...perch votives along its top rail and toss a linen runner on the seat.

Grandma's 6-Layer Salad

Marcella Smith
Poland, OH

A simple, overnight salad recipe.

1 head lettuce, shredded
1 bunch green onions, chopped
1 green pepper, chopped
3/4 c. celery, chopped
8-oz. can sliced water chestnuts
10-oz. pkg. frozen green peas, thawed
1 c. sour cream

1-1/2 c. mayonnaise-type salad dressing
1/2 c. grated Parmesan cheese
8-oz. pkg. shredded Cheddar cheese
6 slices bacon, crisply cooked and crumbled

Layer all vegetables in a 13"x9" pan, pressing down as necessary to make them fit; set aside. Mix sour cream and salad dressing together; spread over vegetables. Sprinkle with Parmesan and Cheddar cheeses, then bacon. Cover and refrigerate overnight. Serves 9 to 12.

Greet family & friends, or even passersby, with pumpkin flowerpots. Fill plump, hollowed-out pumpkins with potted mums then set on porch steps...sure to bring smiles.

Pork Chops with Anise Stuffing

Melanie Lowe
Dover, DE

The anise seed adds a unique, but delicious taste.

1 green pepper, chopped
1/2 c. onion, chopped
3 T. margarine
3 c. bread cubes
1/2 t. seasoned salt

1/2 t. anise seed, crushed
1/4 t. pepper
8-3/4 oz. can corn, drained and
    liquid reserved
6 pork chops

Sauté green pepper and onion in margarine until golden; remove from heat. Add bread cubes, salt, anise and pepper; set aside. Stir corn and 3 tablespoons reserved liquid into stuffing mixture; mix well. Arrange pork chops in an ungreased 13"x9" baking dish; top with stuffing. Bake, covered, at 325 degrees for 1-1/4 hours. Serves 3 to 6.

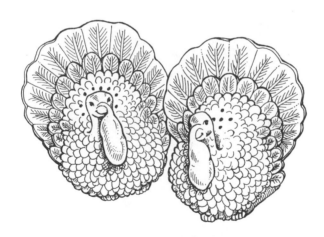

Turkey salt & pepper shakers from the 1950's would brighten any autumn Thanksgiving tabletop.

Sautéed Greens with Pine Nuts

Jackie Gleason
Santa Catalina, CA

You can use sweetened, dried cranberries or golden raisins for a burst of color in this recipe.

1/4 c. raisins
2 cloves garlic, minced
3 T. onion, minced
2 T. oil

1-1/4 lbs. spinach, chopped
3 T. pine nuts
salt and pepper to taste

Place raisins in a bowl and cover with hot water; let stand 10 minutes. Drain; set aside. Sauté garlic and onion in oil until tender; add spinach. Stir-fry for 2 minutes; stir in raisins and nuts. Sprinkle with salt and pepper; cover and cook over low heat for several minutes, until spinach is tender. Serves 4.

A front door wreath offers a warm welcome any time of year.
Top off a simple grapevine wreath with Autumn's
bounty...bittersweet vines, lady apples, yarrow,
ribbon and raffia.

Overnight Rolls

Sandy Lynch
Iroquois, SD

Make these ahead of time and freeze...a great time-saver on Thanksgiving Day!

6 c. warm water
2 c. sugar
1 pkg. active dry yeast
1 c. oil

2 t. salt
4 eggs, beaten
20 c. bread flour

Combine water, sugar and yeast; stir until yeast is dissolved. Add oil, salt, eggs and flour; punch dough down once an hour for 5 hours. Pinch off dough and roll into balls; place on greased baking sheets or in greased round pans. Let stand overnight, uncovered, at room temperature. Bake at 350 degrees 15 to 20 minutes or until golden. Makes 12 dozen.

Autumn placecards...spray paint pressed leaves with a golden paint, then use a permanent pen to add each guest's name.

Grandma Mary's Scalloped Potatoes

Cheryl Wilson
Coshocton, OH

Cream of mushroom or cream of broccoli soup work equally well and sometimes I add slices of cooked Kielbasa or Polish sausage.

8 to 10 potatoes, peeled and
   sliced
4 to 6 slices American cheese

10-3/4 oz. can cream of celery
   soup

Alternate layering potatoes and cheese in a greased 13"x9" baking pan; spread soup over the top. Bake at 375 degrees for 45 minutes, or until potatoes are tender. Serves 4 to 6.

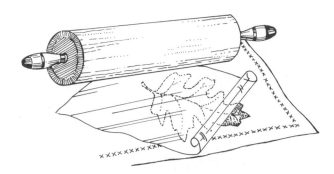

It's easy to make a leaf-print tablecloth. Use a brush to lightly coat a leaf with fabric paint. Place the leaf, paint-side down, onto a linen tablecloth, then press a rolling pin over the leaf several times. Gently lift up the the leaf and repeat using a new leaf. After 24 hours, with the leaf pattern-side down, press the cloth with an iron set at medium high.

Honeyed Pears

Jacqueline Kurtz
Reading, PA

Serve warm for a real treat.

2 16-oz. cans pear halves,
   drained
1/4 c. butter, melted

1/2 c. honey
1 c. macaroons or butter
   cookies, crushed

Arrange pear halves in a single layer in a greased 9"x9" baking pan; set aside. In a small bowl, combine butter with honey; pour over pears. Bake at 350 degrees for 20 minutes. Sprinkle crushed cookies on top and continue baking for an additional 10 minutes. Serves 4.

Give a mirror or picture frame a new look in minutes.
Use hot glue to secure colorful preserved leaves around the
edges...ready in a snap!

Church Festival Salad

Susan Fracker
New Concord, OH

Terrific for potlucks and family gatherings.

1 head red leaf lettuce, chopped
1 head Romaine lettuce, chopped
1 head green leaf lettuce,
  chopped

15-oz. can mandarin oranges,
  drained
1 c. chopped pecans
2 T. sugar

Toss first 4 ingredients together in a serving bowl; set aside. Combine pecans and sugar in a skillet; heat until sugar melts. Stir into lettuce mixture; pour dressing over top and toss to coat. Serves 8.

Dressing:

1/2 c. sugar
2/3 c. oil

1/4 c. red wine vinegar
1 T. soy sauce

Mix all ingredients together in a container with a lid; shake well.

Pretty leaves are
falling down,
Green, orange, yellow
and brown.
Here comes one
colored red,
It landed on my head.

-Unknown

Roast Chicken with Vegetables

Flo Burtnett
Gage, OK

Sometimes I swap out the onions for shallots and potatoes for turnips…still the same delicious recipe, but with a little twist.

3 to 3-1/2 lb. chicken
1 T. plus 1 t. olive oil, divided
1 t. dried thyme
1/2 t. salt
1/2 t. pepper
6 small white onions

6 carrots, cut into 2-inch pieces
6 stalks celery, cut into 2-inch
   pieces
4 potatoes, peeled and cubed

Place chicken in a large shallow roasting pan. Tie the legs together with kitchen string; insert meat thermometer into thickest part of thigh without touching bone. Rub chicken with one teaspoon oil; sprinkle with thyme, salt and pepper. Roast at 475 degrees for 15 minutes. Toss vegetables with remaining oil; arrange around chicken. Reduce oven to 400 degrees; roast for an additional 35 to 45 minutes, until chicken's internal temperature reaches 170 degrees. Serves 6.

Slow-Cooker Stuffing

*Christy Meisner
Waynetown, IN*

My aunt introduced this recipe to me when I began hosting family dinners. It's so easy and very good too!

1/2 c. margarine
1 loaf bread, cubed
1 c. celery, chopped
1 c. onion, chopped

1-1/2 c. canned chicken
14-1/2 oz. can chicken broth
2 10-3/4 oz. cans cream of
   chicken soup

Mix all ingredients together; spoon into a slow cooker. Heat on low setting for 6 hours; increase temperature to high for one additional hour. Serves 6 to 8.

Make a special decorated kids' Thanksgiving table. A Mayflower ship centerpiece can set sail on a map tablecloth, while paper-boat placecards filled with some wrapped candies add to the fun.

Herb-Roasted Turkey

JoAnn

A terrific turkey for dinner and for sandwiches the day after.

14-lb. turkey
1 T. salt
1 t. pepper
18 sprigs fresh thyme, divided
4 onions, peeled and sliced
1 lb. leek, chopped
2 carrots, chopped

4 stalks celery, chopped
3 bay leaves
1 T. peppercorns
1-1/2 c. butter, melted
1 t. fresh sage, chopped
1 t. fresh thyme, chopped
1 t. fresh chives, chopped

Carefully rinse and dry turkey inside and out; set aside giblets. Rub all surfaces with salt and pepper, including cavity. Insert meat thermometer into thickest part of thigh without touching bone. Place 12 sprigs of thyme inside turkey. Place vegetables, bay leaves, remaining thyme, peppercorns and giblets in bottom of large, heavy roasting pan. Place turkey on top of vegetables. Cover opening of cavity with aluminum foil. Brush butter over all surfaces of turkey; sprinkle with sage, thyme and chives. Cover loosely with tent of aluminum foil. Roast at 350 degrees for 2-1/2 hours, undisturbed; remove aluminum foil to let skin brown. Roast and baste every 20 minutes for an additional hour, or until an internal temperature of 180 degrees is reached. Remove from oven. Transfer to platter and cover with aluminum foil; pan juices may be reserved for making gravy. Let turkey rest 15 to 20 minutes before carving. Serves 12 to 14.

Don't forget, if a frozen turkey is planned for the "big day" it needs to begin thawing about 4 days before Thanksgiving…just tuck it in the back of the refrigerator where it's coolest.

Ambrosia

Mary Ann Nemecek
Springfield, IL

Mom made this 5-cup salad in the 1950's and it's still popular today!

1 T. sugar
1 c. sour cream
1 c. miniature marshmallows

1 c. crushed pineapple, drained
1 c. flaked coconut
1 c. mandarin oranges, drained

Stir sugar into sour cream; add remaining ingredients. Stir well; chill.
Makes 5 cups.

Fashion a letter wreath from bittersweet clusters...a large one
for the front door or make tiny placecards. Use bailing wire
to create letter shapes, then wire bittersweet berry clusters
to the form using floral wire.

Apple-Cranberry Salad

Carla Hyde
Fletcher, NC

My Aunt Linda gave me this recipe several years ago after I got married. As a child I remember tasting her yummy dishes and this salad quickly became a favorite for the entire family. It will always be my favorite because it was given by a very special aunt who puts loads of love into everything she makes.

6-oz. pkg. strawberry or
    raspberry gelatin mix
1 c. boiling water
16-oz. can whole cranberry
    sauce

16-oz. can crushed pineapple
1 red apple, cored and diced
1/4 c. chopped nuts
1/4 c. golden raisins

Dissolve gelatin in boiling water. Add cranberry sauce and stir until berries are separated. Add remaining ingredients; chill until set. Makes 12 servings.

Make a chair bouquet from fresh autumn leaves, berry and herb sprigs, clusters of yarrow and mini Indian corn. Wrap together with floral wire, making a hook to slip over the chair, then tie on a ribbon or raffia bow.

Squash, Pecan & Sausage Bake

Marlene Darnell
Newport Beach, CA

Simple to freeze and reheat if you're looking for a make-ahead dish.

2 lbs. yellow squash, sliced
    1/2-inch thick
1/2 c. butter, melted and divided
2 onions, sliced
2 cloves garlic, chopped
1 c. whipping cream
1-1/2 c. bread crumbs, divided
5 eggs, beaten

1 lb. ground sausage, browned,
    crumbled and drained
1-1/2 c. shredded sharp Cheddar
    cheese
1-1/2 c. chopped pecans, divided
salt and pepper to taste

Cover squash with water in a heavy pan; bring to a boil, reduce heat and simmer 30 minutes or until soft. Drain and mash squash. Heat onions in 1/4 cup butter for 5 minutes, then add garlic and heat until soft. Combine onion mixture with squash. Heat cream in another pan, stir in one cup bread crumbs and add mixture to onions and squash. Stir in eggs, sausage, cheese, one cup pecans, salt and pepper. Pour into a greased 2-quart casserole dish. Combine remaining melted butter, pecans and bread crumbs; sprinkle on top and bake, uncovered, for 30 minutes at 350 degrees. Makes 6 to 8 servings.

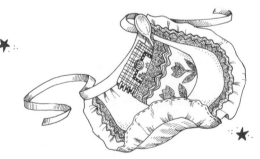

Enjoy favorite recipes this year, but toss in a new one just for fun...you never know, it just might turn out to be a new "favorite!"

Swiss Corn Bake

Debbie Allen
Anaheim, CA

You can always use Cheddar cheese if you'd prefer.

2 10-oz. pkgs. frozen corn,
  cooked and drained
5-oz. can evaporated milk
1 egg, beaten
2 T. onion, chopped
1/2 t. salt

1/8 t. pepper
1 c. shredded Swiss cheese,
  divided
1/2 c. soft bread crumbs
1 T. butter, melted

Combine corn, milk, egg, onion, salt, pepper and 3/4 cup cheese; spread into a buttered 10"x6" baking pan. Toss bread crumbs with butter and remaining cheese; sprinkle over corn mixture. Bake at 350 degrees for 25 minutes. Serves 6.

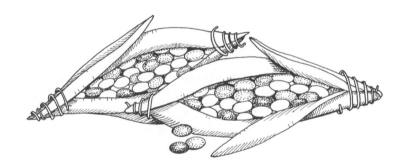

This makes a fun plate decoration for the kids' table. Cut tan or green tissue paper into large leaves that resemble cornhusks. Fill small plastic bags with yellow jelly beans; secure bag with tape. Wrap the "corn husks" around the bag and secure bag ends with floral tape.

Pumpkin Praline Layer Cake

Judy Phelan
Macomb, IL

*I think this is the type of dessert that's so delicious,
it makes your toes curl up!*

1 c. brown sugar, packed
1/2 c. butter
1/4 c. whipping cream
3/4 c. chopped pecans
2 c. all-purpose flour
2 t. pumpkin pie spice
1 t. baking soda
1 t. salt

1-2/3 c. sugar
1 c. oil
4 eggs
2 c. canned pumpkin
1-3/4 c. whipping cream
1/4 c. powdered sugar
1/4 t. vanilla extract
Garnish: pumpkin pie spice

Combine first 3 ingredients in a heavy saucepan over low heat until brown sugar dissolves; stir occasionally. Divide equally between two greased 9" round cake pans. Sprinkle evenly with pecans; let mixture cool slightly. Sift together flour, baking powder, spice, baking soda and salt in a bowl; set aside. Blend sugar, oil and eggs; alternately add pumpkin and reserved dry ingredients. Spoon batter evenly over pecan mixture in cake pans. Place pans on a baking sheet and bake at 350 degrees for 35 to 45 minutes or until centers test clean. Cool cakes in pans on a wire rack for 5 minutes; invert and cool completely on wire rack. Beat whipping cream until soft peaks form; stir in powdered sugar and vanilla. Continue beating until stiff peaks form. To assemble cake, place one layer on a serving plate, praline-side up; spread with whipped topping. Add second layer, praline-side up, and top with remaining whipped cream. Garnish with pumpkin pie spice.
Serves 8.

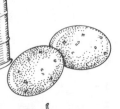

Spicy Gingerbread

Rebecca Chrisman
Citrus Heights, CA

This was one of my favorites when I was a kid. I still make it, and I love the aroma in the kitchen when it's baking!

2 c. all-purpose flour
1 c. molasses
3/4 c. buttermilk
1/2 c. butter, softened
1/2 c. brown sugar, packed

1 t. baking soda
1 t. cinnamon
1 t. ground ginger
1/4 t. ground cloves
1/4 t. salt

Combine all ingredients in a large bowl. Beat with hand mixer on low speed until well blended, scraping sides of bowl frequently. Beat on high speed for 2 additional minutes. Pour into a greased and floured 9" square baking pan. Bake at 325 degrees for 50 to 55 minutes or until wooden pick inserted in center comes out clean. Cool in pan on wire rack about 30 minutes. Cut into squares; serve warm. Makes 16 to 18 servings.

Be sure to have lots of comfy pillows and piles of cozy blankets on hand for early-morning parade watchers and after-dinner nappers!

Pumpkin Pie Squares

Mary Elston Pell
Monroe, LA

A brown sugar oatmeal crust and nutty topping, so yummy!

1 c. all-purpose flour
1/2 c. long-cooking oats, uncooked
1 c. brown sugar, packed and divided
1/2 c. plus 2 T. butter, softened and divided
2 15-oz. cans pumpkin
2 12-oz. cans evaporated milk

4 eggs, beaten
1-1/2 c. sugar
1 T. cornstarch
2 t. cinnamon
1 t. ground ginger
1/2 t. ground cloves
1 t. salt
1/2 c. chopped pecans

Combine flour, oats, 1/2 cup brown sugar and 1/2 cup butter until crumbly. Press into a greased 13"x9" baking pan. Bake at 350 degrees for 20 minutes. Blend pumpkin, evaporated milk, eggs, sugar, cornstarch, cinnamon, ginger, cloves and salt in bowl until smooth; pour over crust. Bake for 45 minutes or until set. Combine pecans with remaining brown sugar and butter; sprinkle over top. Bake for 15 additional minutes. Cool, then chill. Makes 24 servings.

When all the leaves are off the boughs,
And nuts and apples gathered in,
And cornstalks waiting for the cows,
And pumpkins safe in barn and bin,
Then Mother says, "My children dear,
The fields are brown, and autumn flies;
Thanksgiving Day is very near,
And we must make Thanksgiving pies!"

-Unknown

Caramel-Apple Cheesecake

Cathy Park
Wadsworth, OH

Just decadent!

21-oz. can apple pie filling,
    divided
9-inch graham cracker crust
2 8-oz. pkgs. cream cheese,
    softened
2 c. sugar

1/4 t. vanilla extract
2 eggs, beaten
1/4 c. caramel ice cream topping
12 pecan halves
2 T. chopped pecans

Spoon pie filling into crust, reserving 3/4 cup. Blend cream cheese,
sugar and vanilla until smooth; add eggs and mix thoroughly. Pour
over filling; bake at 350 degrees for 35 minutes. Spread reserved
filling on top; spoon caramel topping over filling. Decorate edges with
pecan halves; sprinkle with chopped pecans. Refrigerate until served.
Serves 8.

Don't worry about a specific menu, if friends offer to bring a
dish to share, welcome it! It's fun to see what traditional
foods other families enjoy.

Upside-Down Cranberry Crunch

Jennifer Cizek
Eagle River, AK

The perfect dessert for a happy ending to the day.

3 c. cranberries
1-3/4 c. sugar, divided
1/2 c. chopped pecans
2 eggs

1/2 c. butter, melted
1 c. all-purpose flour
Garnish: whipped cream or ice
   cream

Place cranberries in a greased 8"x8" baking pan. Sprinkle with 3/4 cup sugar and pecans. In a mixing bowl, blend together eggs, butter, flour and remaining sugar until smooth. Spread over cranberry mixture. Bake at 325 degrees for one hour or until a toothpick inserted near the center comes out clean. Run knife around edges of pan; immediately invert onto a serving plate. Serve with whipped cream or ice cream. Makes 8 servings.

Capture all those holiday memories for scrapbooks to be treasured. Tuck in handwritten recipe cards, early-morning snapshots of Mom in the kitchen, a guest list and even after-dinner nappers.

Pumpkin Nut Cups

Pat Habiger
Spearville, KS

So tiny and fun to make...you can't stop nibbling on them!

1/2 c. butter, softened
3-oz. pkg. cream cheese,
   softened
1 c. all-purpose flour
3/4 c. brown sugar, packed and
   divided
1/4 c. canned pumpkin
1 egg yolk

1 T. half-and-half
1 T. plus 4 t. butter, melted
1/4 t. rum extract
1 t. vanilla extract
1/8 t. cinnamon
1/8 t. nutmeg
1/2 c. chopped pecans

In a medium mixing bowl, blend 1/2 cup butter and cream cheese with an electric mixer until well blended; stir in flour. Divide dough into 24 balls, one inch in diameter, and press the dough evenly into the bottoms and up sides of twenty-four, 1-3/4 inch muffin cups. Bake at 325 degrees for 10 minutes. Combine 1/2 cup brown sugar, pumpkin, egg yolk, half-and-half, 4 teaspoons butter, extracts, cinnamon and nutmeg; spoon evenly into warm dough cups. Stir together nuts with remaining brown sugar and butter; sprinkle over pumpkin mixture. Bake for 25 additional minutes. Cool in pans for 10 minutes; loosen and remove from pans. Serve warm or cool. Makes 2 dozen.

Before dinner, take time to hold hands and ask everyone at the table to share what they're thankful for...some of the sweetest memories will be made.

Index

Index

Mains

Salads

Sandwiches

Index

We've cooked up a whole collection of Gooseberry Patch® books!

Have a taste for more? Call us toll-free at

1-800-854-6673

We'll send you our latest catalog filled with snowmen, Santas, ornaments, candles, cookie cutters, gourmet goodies, calendars, giftwrap, pottery, collectibles and MORE...including our best-selling cookbooks!

Phone us:
1·800·854·6673

Fax us:
1·740·363·7225

Visit our website:
www.gooseberrypatch.com

Send us your favorite recipe!

and the memory that makes it special for you! If we select your recipe for a brand new **Gooseberry Patch** cookbook, your name will appear right along with it...and you'll receive a FREE copy of the book! Mail to:

Vickie & Jo Ann
Gooseberry Patch, Dept. Book
600 London Road
Delaware, Ohio 43015

*Please include the number of servings and all other necessary information!

harvest moon · ☽ · songs & laughter ♡ hayrides

frosty meadows

the snap of a football ⬭ the rustle of leaves

gather 'round · the rustle of leaves

fresh picked apples · crackling fires